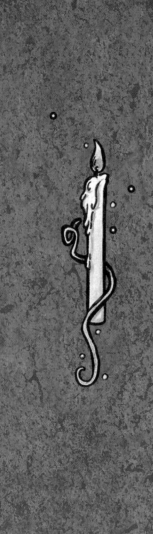

Bless this book
In the name of the God and the Goddess
Who guide my feet on the Path of Beauty
Let it be filled with wisdom and knowledge
Let me use it only for good
Let me share it with those who need it
Let it help me grow in my Craft
And in my life
So mote it be

Bobbie Hodges

*D*eborah Blake is the author of over a dozen books on modern Witchcraft, including *The Little Book of Cat Magic* and *Everyday Witchcraft,* as well as the acclaimed *Everyday Witch Tarot* and *Everyday Witch Oracle* decks. She has also written three paranormal romance and urban fantasy series for Berkley, and her new cozy mystery series launches with *Furbidden Fatality* in 2021. Deborah lives in a 130-year-old farmhouse in upstate New York with numerous cats who supervise all her activities, both magical and mundane. She can be found at

DEBORAHBLAKEAUTHOR.COM

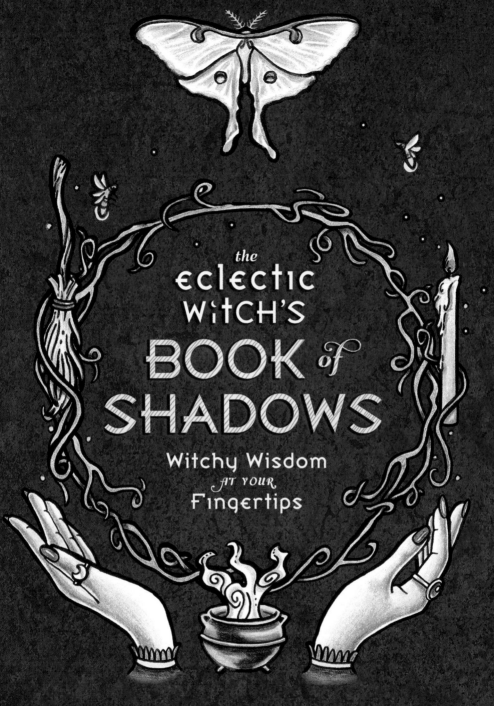

the

eclectic witch's

BOOK of
SHADOWS

Witchy Wisdom
AT YOUR
Fingertips

DEBORAH BLAKE

Llewellyn Publications
WOODBURY, MINNESOTA

FIRST EDITION
Fourth Printing, 2023

Art direction by Lynne Menturweck and Shira Atakpu
Book design, layout, and edit by Rebecca Zins
Cover design by Shira Atakpu
Cover and interior illustrations by Mickie Mueller

*Llewellyn Publications is a registered trademark
of Llewellyn Worldwide Ltd.*

Library of Congress Cataloging-in-Publication Data
Names: Blake, Deborah, author.
Title: The eclectic witch's book of shadows : witchy wisdom at your
   fingertips / Deborah Blake.
Description: First edition. | Woodbury, Minnesota: Llewellyn Publications,
   [2021] | Summary: "This beginner-friendly guide is modeled on a
   traditional Wiccan Book of Shadows but is flexible enough to be
   personalized. With sections on herbs, stones, spells, rituals, candle
   magic, divination, correspondences, magical recipes, and more, this book
   makes practicing Witchcraft easier, simpler, and more fun"—Provided by
   publisher.
Identifiers: LCCN 2021005118 (print) | LCCN 2021005119 (ebook) | ISBN
   9780738765327 (hardcover) | ISBN 9780738765563 (ebook)
Subjects: LCSH: Witchcraft.
Classification: LCC BF1566 .B53434 2021 (print) | LCC BF1566 (ebook) |
   DDC 133.4/3—dc23
LC record available at https://lccn.loc.gov/2021005118
LC ebook record available at https://lccn.loc.gov/2021005119

Llewellyn Publications
A Division of Llewellyn Worldwide Ltd.
2143 Wooddale Drive
Woodbury, MN 55125-2989

www.llewellyn.com

Printed in China

Contents

Introduction...1

Herbs 7

contents

Stones..37

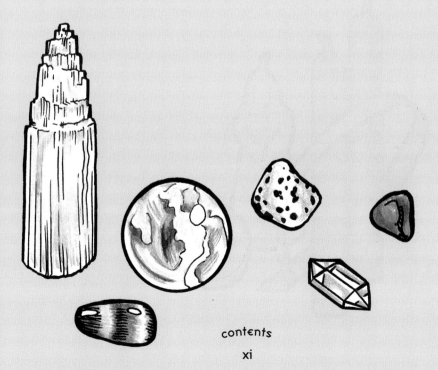

contents

Candles..65

Magical Recipes..................................81

contents

Divination...105

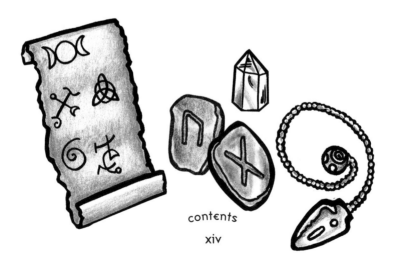

Gods and Goddesses.................... 123

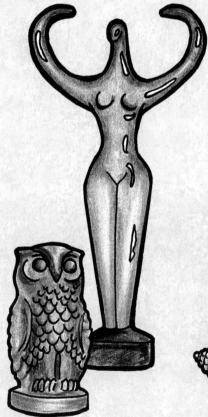

Invocations and Quarter Calls........141

Spells 169

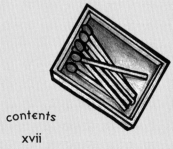

Correspondences

Introduction

itches use many tools in the practice of their Craft. What these tools consist of can vary widely from witch to witch. For some, the athame and the cauldron are vital, symbolizing the God and the Goddess and practical for directing energy and either burning or heating things in respectively. For others, it might be a wand, a staff, a broom, an assortment of crystals, or herbs or candles—maybe all of the above. And why not? Anything that is useful and boosts your magical power is worth having; if it is beautiful, that's a bonus.

The tools that mean something to us on a personal and emotional level are also the ones that hold the most power. Whether it is a special pentacle necklace gifted to you by a friend, that piece of rose quartz that called to you during a time when you needed its calming aura, or even the simple athame you bought when you first realized you were a witch, the tools that are the most deeply *yours* are the ones that mean the most. They personify your magic, and over time and use, they become a part of you.

There is no tool more personal than a witch's Book of Shadows. Sometimes called a grimoire, a Book of Shadows contains a witch's magical information and the knowledge she or he gains over years of practice. Not every witch has one, and one Book of Shadows can look very different from another. As with everything else in Witchcraft, there is no one "right way" to create one or use one, no matter what you might have been told.

Keep in mind that the name "Book of Shadows" is relatively new, almost certainly originating with Gerald Gardner in the 1940s. The grimoire, or book of magic, however, goes quite deep into history, although that particular name is European in origin. There have been magical books dating back as far as the Library of Alexandria, the Greeks and Romans, the ancient Jews, and the Gnostic sects of early Christianity. Certainly the possession of such a book could have gotten you killed during the grim years of the witch hunts.

Thankfully, these days most of us can add a Book of Shadows to our collection of Witchcraft tools without fear of being burned at the stake, although not everyone is going to leave theirs out where others can see it. (Mine is old, but it definitely doesn't date back to the Library of Alexandria!)

In the early days of Wicca, a coven usually had a main Book of Shadows, and new initiates were allowed to copy the information it held into their own personal books, which they then added to as they pursued their studies. They were sworn to secrecy, and the secrets of the coven's magic were not to be shared with outsiders.

These days a coven might still have a group Book of Shadows, whether or not it is a secret. My group Blue Moon Circle does, although it is a fairly simple collection of our rituals along with some photos taken over the years (including vacations we took together), a copy of "The Charge of the Goddess," and the names of each member who has been a part of Blue Moon Circle written on the inside front cover. It is as much a record of our journey together as it is a book of magic, and it brings back amazing memories whenever I look at it.

It is not, however, a deep dark secret, nor (I hate to admit it) very well organized. It doesn't have beautiful hand-drawn illustrations because my artistic skills are, shall we say, rudimentary at best. And it isn't even written out by hand because my handwriting is so appalling, we'd never be able to read it later. So I type up the spells and rituals—sometimes using a pretty font, so that must count for something, right?—and tape them into the book. We're modern eclectic witches, people. We do whatever works!

For the most part, a Book of Shadows is created and used by an individual witch. Traditionally, such books were always supposed to be handwritten. It was thought that writing out the spells and information in your own handwriting gave them more power. Does it? Perhaps, and certainly if you have the time, the inclination, and decent penmanship, that's a great way to go. But with the increased use of computers, not to mention the publication of books like the one you are currently holding in your hands, it has become more common to either type out your lists and spells and recipes or else use a book written by someone else.

This book is meant to take the place of a Book of Shadows you have to start from scratch, although there are plenty of blank pages so you can add your own notes as you follow the journey that is your life in the Craft. I called it *The Eclectic Witch's Book of Shadows* because that is how I think of myself: as a witch who uses bits of this and that to make up my own personal Witchcraft journey. Whether you are a Wiccan, an eclectic witch, or anything in between, I hope that you will find this Book of Shadows useful, entertaining, and, of course, magical.

How to Use This Book

As with any of my books, and all magical tools really, the answer to this question is "whichever way works best for you." There is no one right approach to practicing Witchcraft, and therefore no one right way to use a Book of Shadows. For those who are new to the Craft, it might be helpful to start at the beginning and work through the book in order, learning as you go. Those who have been practicing for some time may wish to simply jump from section to section, using whichever bit is the most helpful for whatever magical workings you are doing at the time.

For instance, if you are experimenting with magical herbs, you might go to that section and see what information I have to share—but you don't need to stop there. Once you start doing work of your own, you can add notes on what worked or didn't, which herbs you were most drawn to, and so on. You can simply use the book as-is, of course, but you also have the opportunity to truly make this into your own Book of Shadows by writing down the results of your personal magical practice. *Hint:* if you use a journal page for a spell or a note, you can write what it was on the dotted line in the table of contents.

Which stones seem the most effective for prosperity or healing? Are there spells that seem to work for you every time? Which gods and goddesses do you connect to most, and why? This is *your* Book of Shadows. Use it for exploration, for learning, for practice, or just to read out of general interest—there is no right or wrong way, simply what works for you.

Feel free to write and draw on the pages, too!

This is your book—
fill it with your magic!
♡

Herbs

*H*erbs are one of the most valuable tools in a witch's bag of tricks. Luckily, most of them are also inexpensive and easy to find. Even the exotic-sounding "eye of newt" was just another name for mustard seed, which might already be in your kitchen cupboard. Ceremonial magicians may use mandrake root, but most of us witches are just as well served by rosemary and lavender.

In fact, many of the herbs and plants used in magical work are multipurpose and also can be used for healing and cooking, among other things. This makes mixing magic and the mundane easy, since you can add a bit of herbal magic to your meal, cup of tea, or bath.

Our witchy predecessors were often herbalists and healers who either grew or foraged for many of their magical ingredients. Their skill was valued by those who knew they could be relied upon for help with matters of the body, heart, or spirit, and this knowledge was sometimes passed down through families or by apprenticeship.

Back in those days, much of the learning was probably taught by example, but sometimes information was shared through grimoires or even simple household books that were probably filled with drawings of the herbs and prized methods for charms, potions, and recipes. They may not have called themselves witches, but they were Pagans who lived on and valued the land, and that's good enough for me.

These days, witches are more likely to be self-taught, unless they have both the inclination to be part of a coven and the good fortune to be able to find one nearby. The herbal knowledge in our own modern grimoires or Books of Shadows is sometimes gleaned from books or trial and error or even (*shhh…*) the internet. But we still use herbs as one of the core elements of a Witchcraft practice, and they are the perfect place to start a Book of Shadows.

herbs

Some of My Favorite Herbs and Their Uses

*Keep in mind that for magical purposes, the
word "herb" is used for pretty much any kind of
plant, so that includes what we'd normally consider
to be an herb (like rosemary or thyme) as well as fruits, trees,
shrubs, and even so-called weeds like dandelion or burdock.*

Apple: *Blossoms, fruit, and wood.* Primarily used for love
and healing magic, although the wood makes a nice
wand and the cider is a great "ale" for cakes and ale
at the end of a ritual, especially one that
takes place in the fall. Apples are
particularly witchy because if you slice
one crosswise, you will see the shape
of a pentacle inside. For simple love
magic, try baking an apple pie and
adding cinnamon, which is associated
with passion.

Basil: *Leaves.* Used for love, protection, prosperity, and
(theoretically) exorcism. (I don't have any experience
with that last one, but you could certainly use it to try
banishing negative emotions.) Easily used in cooking,
like my recipe for prosperity pesto (see page 234),
which I make with walnuts (fertility) instead of pine
nuts. As a dried herb, basil also works well when
added to sachets or magical mixes.

Calendula: *Flowers.* Also known as marigold. Often used by herbalists for its healing properties but also grown by many folks as an ornamental. In magic it can be used for healing, love, and to boost psychic abilities. I like to use the dried flowers in healing sachets, although I also grow them in my garden just because they're pretty.

Catnip: *Leaves, flowers.* Love, happiness, beauty, sleep, calm, connection with cats. While more often associated with felines than with humans, catnip (which is a member of the prolific mint family) has healing qualities for people as well. Magically, you can use it in sachets for sleep, calm, and love, but be prepared to share them with your cats if you have any. It is also useful in cat magic, especially a spell to find a familiar.

herbs

Chamomile: *Flowers.* Peace, sleep, love, prosperity, protection. This is one of my favorite herbs to use in sleep or calming sachets. It is also a traditional healing tea that can be used for either of those purposes, so you can bless and consecrate some chamomile on the night of the full moon and then drink it as a tea when you need it.

Cinnamon: *Bark.* Prosperity, success, passion, love, lust, healing, protection, power, psychic ability, spirituality. Who would have thought that the simple cinnamon in your cupboard would have so many magical uses? Cinnamon is especially useful in love and prosperity mixtures and can easily be added to food. Actually a spice that comes from the inner bark of an evergreen tree, cinnamon is usually found in its powdered form, but I like to use cinnamon sticks (long chunks that haven't been ground up) in charm bags, magical mixes, and even as a miniature wand to stir the Yule wassail.

Dill: *Leaves, flowers, and seeds.* Love, protection, prosperity. Magical prosperity pickles? Sure, why not? Dill is a tall plant that is used both for its delicate-looking thin green leaves and then, later in the season, the flowering heads filled with seeds that are used to flavor pickles and other foods. It is easy to grow and can be used fresh or dried. For a boost of prosperity, I toss the fresh herb in my salads in early summer and add it to various magical mixes later in the year in its dried form.

Eucalyptus: *Leaves.* Healing and protection. Eucalyptus is a powerful healing herb, whether you are using the dried leaves or the essential oil. It has a strong, pungent odor and can be quite powerful, so it is best used in small amounts. The oil can be added to healing mixtures or the leaves placed in sachets or poppets intended for healing use.

Garlic: *Bulb.* Healing, protection. As anyone who has ever eaten it knows, garlic is a strong-smelling herb that will chase away prospective dates and possibly vampires. But in magical work, its protective properties will definitely work for your benefit. You can use whole cloves in protection sachets or powdered dry garlic in spell mixtures. (I don't suggest putting those under your pillow, though.) It is also used for healing and can be added to food if you are doing kitchen witchery. Magical chicken soup for a cold? You bet! Just remember to focus on its healing potential as you use it.

Geranium: *Flowers, leaves.* Love, healing, protection. Geraniums are a pretty and easy-to-grow plant that comes in a range of colors, red and pink being among the most common. The plants themselves can act as protection for the home, and the flowers can be picked and added to sachets or other magical preparations. Rose geranium in particular has very pleasantly scented leaves and makes a lovely essential oil. (Note that geranium essential oil and rose geranium essential oil will have different scents; they are both useful for love and protection work, but the rose geranium in particular is known for its calming and healing properties.)

Ginger: *Root.* Power, energy, prosperity, success, love (especially the passionate type). Ginger is a fiery herb that lends its heat and power to any spell you use it in. It can be used in the powdered form in magical mixtures, or pieces of the whole root can be sliced and added to food or charm bags.

Most of the herbs I've listed are perfectly safe for cats and dogs, but you always want to use caution if you are using plants around animals. Keep in mind that they are often attracted to the smell of herbs and will chew on live plants and gnaw through plastic bags to get to dried herbs.

Lavender: *Flowers.* Love, sleep, happiness, purification, healing, peace. Lavender is a beautiful and strongly scented flower with many magical uses. If you have a garden, it is lovely to cut the fresh flowers and place them on your altar. For most, however, the dried version will have to do. My group often follows the traditional practice of tossing lavender into the Midsummer bonfire as a sacrifice to the Goddess. I also use the herb in sachets for healing and peace, and tuck one under my pillow to help me sleep. It makes a wonderful incense, and the essential oil is easy to use in magical baths or sprays.

Lemon: *Juice, peel.* Purification, cleansing, love, energy. All the citruses (specifically lemon, orange, and grapefruit) have similar magical properties, but lemon in particular is good for any purification or cleansing work. Add a few drops to your mop water for a magical boost to your housework, especially if you are doing spring cleaning. The dried peel can be added to sachets and charm bags for love or purification, and the essential oil is perfect for room sprays that are intended to purify your space and boost your energy.

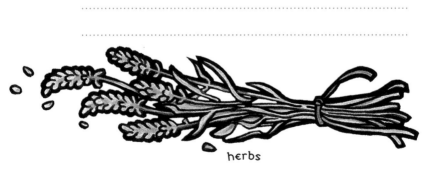

herbs

Lemon Balm: *Leaves*. Healing, happiness, calm, love. Lemon balm is a member of the mint family and will grow prolifically in a garden. It is known for its ability to attract bees and is sacred to Artemis and Diana. Lemon balm can be made into a magical tea to boost the mood or calm a troubled spirit, and the leaves or essential oil are particularly helpful in spell mixtures to deal with sleep, anxiety, or depression.

Mugwort: *Leaves*. Psychic powers, protection, divination, dreaming, astral projection. Mugwort's most common use is in a dream sachet, which, when tucked under one's pillow, is said to aid in prophetic dreaming. It is also used in incenses and drunk in teas to boost the user's powers of divination. While not as dangerous as the hallucinogenic herbs employed by earlier witches, some people can find mugwort overwhelming, and it should be used with caution if you have no previous experience with it.

Parsley: *Leaves*. Protection and purification. Parsley isn't considered to be one of the more powerful magical herbs, but I like it because it is so easy to add to foods if you are doing kitchen witchery. If you are already making a dish with the magical intent of protection or purification, why not toss in a little parsley for a magical boost?

Peppermint: *Leaves*. Healing, purification, love, prosperity, abundance, psychic powers. Peppermint has traditionally been used for healing work, either as a tea or by rubbing the leaves over the affected area. In herbal medicine it is used both for upset stomachs and headaches, so this makes sense. The leaves or a few drops of essential oil can be sprinkled in vulnerable areas to keep away pests and added to wash water when you are housecleaning or mopping. I like to use it in prosperity work. As a member of the mint family, peppermint spreads and grows exuberantly, making it the perfect symbol for abundance.

Rose: *Petals and hips (rose hips are the fruit of the plant).* Love, healing, protection, divination. Roses are useful in healing work, but their most common association—magically and otherwise—is with love. If you are making a love sachet or any kind of love magic mixture, you will definitely want to add rose petals. You can use a fresh rose or roses, or the dried petals. If doing healing work, you may want to use rose hips, which are high in vitamin C and can be made into a healing tea. If someone you love (romantically or not) gives you roses, hang them upside down to dry and keep the petals for magical work. Different colors of roses can also be used for varying kinds of magic, such as red for passion and pink for friendship.

Rosemary: *Leaves.* Healing, protection, love, conscious mind and memory, purification. Rosemary is an all-around hardworking magical herb. It is associated with protection, and people used to plant rosemary bushes outside their homes to keep them safe from thieves and maintain the health of those in the household. (You can use small potted plants or a rosemary wreath instead.) It boosts all mental abilities, so you can burn rosemary incense if you have to study for a test. A common saying is "rosemary for remembrance," which refers not only to its mind-sharpening gifts but also its use in rituals to honor the dead. It is my favorite protection herb, and I use it in all my charm bags and magical kits for that purpose.

* add rosemary essential oil to diffuser when I need to focus

herbs

Sage: *Leaves*. Protection, purification, wisdom, long life. Probably best known for its use in sage smudge sticks, which are used to purify both people and spaces. Sage sticks are usually made from white sage, which grows in desert conditions and is stronger in flavor and aroma than the common culinary sage most of us have in our kitchens. Regular culinary sage can be used both in cooking and magic. Sage is easy to grow in the garden or on a windowsill, so you can pluck a leaf or two and add it to your food. Dried sage can be used in protection charm bags or mixes. If eaten regularly, the herb was said to impart long life and also make one wise. (This makes sense, since "sage" is another word for a wise person.)

Thyme: *Leaves*. Purification, healing, psychic ability, love, sleep. Thyme is another herb that is easy to grow in the garden (or even places where you walk, since it makes a sweet-smelling ground cover) or on a kitchen windowsill. Fresh or dried thyme can be used in various magical applications. It can be burned to purify a space before magical work or added to healing baths, teas, or magical mixes. It is said that if you place it under your pillow, it will cure nightmares. Lore has it that if a woman wears thyme in her hair, she will be irresistible—but I have to wonder if people are just staring at her because she has a plant in her hair.

Yarrow: *Leaves and flowers*. Courage, love, protection, psychic ability, exorcism. Yarrow is a flowering herb that can often be found growing wild, and it is a pretty addition to an herb garden, witchy or otherwise. It has traditionally been used in protection and love spells and was said to make love last for at least seven years. (After year eight, you're on your own.) It can be made into a tea, dried and added to charm bags or decorations, or placed in a vase as a fresh bouquet when it is in season. You can use its exorcism powers to help drive out negativity from your home.

• • • • • • • •

There are many, many, MANY more herbs than I have listed here, some of which are quite commonly used for Witchcraft. Some of them I don't use because I don't like the smell or I've simply found more readily available herbs that work for me just as well. And frankly, I don't have the space or the money to stock every kind of herb there is, so I tend to pick the ones I can also use for medicinal or culinary purposes or that I can utilize for multiple magical needs. But this is your Book of Shadows, so feel free to add notes on any other herbs you wish to add to your own list or keep track of which ones seem to work the best for you.

herbs

Yarrow: A Cautionary Tale

Yarrow is a commonly used magical herb, and it can also be quite useful for healing applications. But I never use it because I'm highly allergic to it. I found out by accident, a number of years before I became a witch, when I was attending a wedding in a meadow filled with the stuff and someone recommended making a tea for some ailment I had. So I walked around the meadow picking the pretty white flowers on their long stalks and after a while, I noticed that my hands were itching. When I looked down, I realized that I had huge blisters—the size of quarters—coming out all over my palms where I'd been holding the yarrow. Needless to say, I was glad I found out before I made it into a tea and drank it! The lesson here is that just because something is an herb, that doesn't mean it is safe. Even the ones that aren't normally considered dangerous can be harmful if you happen to be sensitive to them. Please use caution when dealing with an herb that is new to you, especially if you plan to ingest it. Yarrow. That's all I'm saying.

How to Use Herbs

The short answer, of course, is "any way you want to." They really are incredibly flexible. Most herbs not only can be used both fresh and dried, they also are available as essential oils and incense and can have a place in your house or garden as living plants. Each form has its own advantages; some herbs work better dried, while others may be at their best when they are newly picked. Which form you use may also depend on the application you have in mind, too. For instance, while you might use fresh rose petals in a bath, for a shower spray you would undoubtedly want the essential oil.

In general spellwork, I often use the fresh herb if I have it and otherwise make do with the dried. I like the powerful energy that comes from the living plant (which is another reason to have a few on your windowsill or in your yard), but there are only so many plants I can grow myself. Plus, I live in a part of the country where the growing season is limited.

There are some exceptions, of course. For instance, there is no such thing as fresh cinnamon, at least not where most of us live. And if I am using sage in a spell, I might use either form, but if I want to use a sage wand for purification, that calls for white sage that already has been bundled in its dry form, rather than the culinary sage I grow in my garden. (Although I have been known to dry that at the end of the season and throw it into a bonfire.)

There is no wrong way. If you don't happen to have a green thumb or the inclination to grow your own herbs, buying dried herbs from a magical supplier or the local health food store is perfectly acceptable. You can, of course, use the dried herbs found in the seasoning section of your grocery store, but they come in tiny containers and tend to be expensive compared to buying them in bulk. Also, some of them have been irradiated to preserve them, and that's not exactly the kind of energy we're looking for.

Some witches store their magical herbs with the rest of their magical supplies, while others simply grab what they need out of the kitchen. I do a little of both, although once I have blessed and consecrated an herbal mixture for magical use, I put it in a special container and keep it separate. If you have the space and the inclination, it can be fun to have a cabinet or shelf lined with decorative jars filled with magical ingredients for potions, ointments, spell mixtures, teas, and more.

....

....

....

....

....

....

....

....

....

....

....

....

....

....

....

....

....

Potions: Potion is really just a fancy word for an infusion or decoction—which are both fancy words for "just add hot water." Potions are more likely to be produced ahead of time, have the herbs strained out, and then be left to cool before they are used. You might, for instance, make a protection potion or infusion with a number of herbs that are good for that purpose, and then use a few drops of the resulting liquid during magical work later on by adding them to a bath, to cleaning water, anointing yourself with it during spellwork, and so on. Potions are usually blessed or otherwise infused with magic as they are being made, or else they are consecrated on the altar afterward.

Witch's Flying Ointment

In today's world, we know lots of fascinating herbs that were traditionally associated with Witchcraft and herbal medicine are just too dangerous to use. It isn't that they're not powerful—it is that they are too powerful to mess around with, and there are plenty of safer alternatives. Some of these herbs are thought to be the ingredients for the so-called witch's flying ointment, which was used to aid in astral projection, in theory so witches could meet up without having to leave the safety of their home.

Instead of using belladonna, datura, hemlock, foxglove, or aconite, today's witches who wish to experiment with altered states of consciousness or astral projection may use lavender for relaxation or rosemary to sharpen the conscious mind. Used in addition to drumming or recorded ocean sounds, meditation techniques, and trance work, it is still possible to achieve magical travel without the risks of dangerous herbs.

Teas: Teas, on the other hand, are usually created with the intention of drinking them right away. The difference between magical teas and the nice English Breakfast tea you had this morning is intent. As you steep your herbs, you concentrate on whatever your magical intention is (like healing) and use herbs that are magically associated with that task. Needless to say, teas should only be made with herbs that are safe for consumption, and you will probably want to stick to ones that taste good!

Healing Tea

Place a half teaspoon each of fresh or dried peppermint leaves and chamomile flowers inside a tea ball or muslin bag, along with a pinch of dried ginger or a slice of fresh ginger root. Hold the ball or bag in your hands for a moment and concentrate on your intention of healing. Place the herbs in a mug or teapot and cover with hot water. Allow the tea to steep for three to five minutes, depending on how strong you want it to taste. Then remove the herbs (if you used a teapot, pour the liquid into a mug). Hold the mug up and say, "Goddess, bless this tea with the power of healing." Drink it slowly, feeling the herbs' power filling your body.

Most of all, remember to be kind to yourself.
–Blake

Ointments, creams, and salves: This is an application most often used for healing herbs and is less popular than it used to be. Basically, you heat the herbs with some form of fat—this can be anything from lard to olive oil to cocoa butter—and then strain the herbs out. Some people add beeswax as well. Once they are finished, they can be blessed for magical work such as healing or calming.

Baths: Magical baths are a wonderful way to submerge yourself in enchanted intentions since the energy of the plants spreads throughout the water as you soak it in. Herbs can be enclosed in a cloth (a sachet) or you can use a few drops of a potion you made ahead of time. Essential oils also work well in the bath, although you want to be careful to use them sparingly since they can be quite powerful. In some cases, when it won't be too messy (like rose petals, which are large), you can actually float the herbs right on the surface of the water. Adding sea salt to your magical bath will give it a boost as well, since it represents both earth and water elements.

....

....

....

....

Beauty Bath

To enhance the beauty of your being both inside and out, place lavender flowers and rose petals in a small muslin bag or sprinkle them on the bath water. Alternately, you can place three drops of lavender essential oil and three drops of rose essential oil into the water, then mix them in by swirling your hand through the water in a clockwise (deosil) direction. Soak in the water for as long as is comfortable, and envision yourself glowing with beauty from the inside out.

herbs

Shower sprays: Not everyone has a tub or the time to take a bath every time they need a magical boost. Magical sprays are easy to make and also can be used as room sprays. You can either use a few drops of any potion you have made up or use essential oils. I like to make sprays for healing, cleansing, or protection to use around the house, and the shower spray I use in the morning has herbs for prosperity, energy, and healing all mixed together to start my day off right (if you must know, it's a mixture of rosemary, peppermint, geranium, and grapefruit essential oils mixed with water).

Incense: Some witches make their own incense using powdered herbs that are usually mixed with some kind of binder and then burned on a charcoal disk. Be aware that these tend to be strong-smelling and smoky, and they are not suitable for use inside unless you have good ventilation. On the occasions I use incense, I tend to stick to something premade using essential oils. (Fragrance oils, which are in many incenses, are artificial and don't have the energy of the plants they are supposed to smell like.) Alternately, if I am having a ritual that involves a bonfire outside, I often throw herbs in the fire, which can smell absolutely heavenly.

Sachets, charm bags, and poppets: These are all forms of magic that use cloth to enclose various magical ingredients, often including herbs. There is more detail on them later in the book.

herbs

dusty miller

herbs

Drying Herbs

There are a number of ways to dry herbs for use later. The simplest method, used by our ancestors, was to hang them upside down in bunches in a dry area. This is how it has always been done. You can also dry them slowly in your oven or more quickly—like in two minutes—in your microwave. While this may seem very modern and un-witchy, it actually preserves much of the color and vigor of the plant.

mugwort

thyme

herbs

34

bay leaves

Stones

lmost as useful to the witch as herbs (and way more shiny), gemstones and crystals can be a vital part of the magical tool kit. They can be used for everything from healing to protection and a whole lot more. Plus, many of them are beautiful, and who couldn't benefit from having more beauty in their life?

I must confess, I probably have more stones than your average witch. Maybe it has to do with being a Taurus, which is one of the earth signs. Maybe I need the extra grounding one can get from being surrounded by rocks. (Almost definitely.) It could be because I also make gemstone jewelry, so I clearly have an affinity for pretty stones. Either way, I have *a lot* of stones.

But that doesn't mean you have to go out and buy one of every kind of rock there is. There are a few essential gemstones and crystals that between them can cover virtually every magical need, and not all of them are fancy or expensive. Remember, too, that you don't necessarily have to own a giant ten-pound amethyst cluster (although I won't judge you if you do). In most cases, small tumbled versions or reasonably sized crystals will do. If you can't afford the more expensive ones, sometimes there is a less pricy alternative to the more costly stones that has the same magical properties.

Not all stones are created equal, though. If you can, it is best to pick up the stones and hold them, getting a feel for their energy and whether or not that energy resonates with you. I realize that not everyone has a store in their area that sells crystals, or a gem show nearby, or any other venue that gives you the opportunity to "meet" the rocks in person, but if you can, this is definitely the best way to find the stones that will best suit your own magical work.

If you don't have any other choice, you can look at stones online and see if any of them really jump out at you. But if you can visit with them in person, so much the better. If you can pick them up and get a feel for their energy and whether or not they feel right to you, that increases the chances of your ending up with the stone that suits your own vibrations, for lack of a better term. I can't tell you how many times I have stood in front of a display of gemstones at a spiritual arts fair or a shop and looked at one beautiful piece after another, only to realize that I had unconsciously picked one up and didn't want to let it go. Those are the stones that come home with me.

There can be a huge variation between stones of the same type, both visually and energetically. If you are looking for a rose quartz that will be calming, for instance, you may have to handle ten or twenty pieces before you find the one that is right for you—or you may be drawn to the one you need straight off.

Don't worry if this sounds too complicated. It doesn't have to be. Some people just buy or are gifted stones of the kind they want, and it works out just fine. But if you have the chance to experiment, you might find the results intriguing.

Stones and crystals can bring a lot of power to magical work, helping to focus your energy and intent on whatever it is you are trying to achieve. Like herbs, stones tend to have particular magical associations, but remember that these kinds of associations are general guidelines and not hard-and-fast rules.

If your intuition says to use rose quartz for grounding even though that isn't one of the things it is usually supposed to be good for, absolutely follow your gut. And as with the section on herbs, feel free to use this book's blank and ruled pages to add any stones you use that haven't already been included here, or notes on your experiences with any of the stones you work with.

....

....

....

....

....

....

....

....

....

....

....

....

....

....

....

....

....

stones

stones

40

Some of My Favorite Stones and Their Magical Uses

Agate (various colors): *Love, healing, protection, courage, and more.* Agate is one of the most common stones there is. It is inexpensive and available in many colors, and you may wish to use different types for different magical needs. As with most stones, the color tends to dictate each agate's specialty. Some of the better known are black agate, which is used for protection; blue lace agate, which is associated with peace and calm; and moss or tree agates for gardeners and prosperity.

Amber (pale yellow to deep orange): *Healing, protection, strength, luck, love, magic.* Not actually a gemstone at all, amber is the fossilized resin of the ancient ancestors of our pine trees. Despite this, it is one of the most valuable "stones" in a witch's collection. In some cultures amber was hung around a child's neck or in their bedroom for protection. It is thought to lend power to all magical workings. Perhaps it is so powerful because of how old it is. Amber is getting harder to find and therefore more expensive, but it is still worth having some in your collection. You are most likely to find amber in small chunks or beads, so you may want to consider using it in jewelry.

Amethyst (pale lavender to deep purple): *Love, healing, psychic ability, spirit, calm, happiness, protection, dreams.* A form of quartz, amethyst is one of those stones that is good for almost everything. Although it can be pricier than some other stones, it is nice to have at least a small tumbled stone or crystal in your magical tool kit. It is one of the most spiritual stones there is. Amethyst is used to focus or increase psychic ability, commune with deity and higher self, quiet nightmares, and produce prophetic dreams. It is associated with calm, healing, courage, and love, as well as protection. Some tarot readers, including me, keep a small amethyst crystal tucked in with their deck to clear the energy and boost the power of the one reading the cards.

Aventurine (green): *Prosperity, healing, creativity, luck.* Aventurine is a pretty green type of quartz that can vary in hue from light to dark. It looks a bit like jade, but it is much less expensive. (It also comes in a few other colors, like peach, but in general when people talk about the stone, they mean the green form.) I primarily use aventurine in magical work that focuses on money or good luck, but it is also useful for healing and anything to do with mental sharpness.

Carnelian (orange to red): *Courage, strength, protection, healing, peace, energy, sexuality.* A form of chalcedony that was widely used in Egypt and Rome. This stone can vary in color, but my favorite is the more vivid red, which I find very beautiful. Carnelian is used by those who speak in public and need a boost of courage and confidence. It is perfect for magical protection work as well as to counter negativity and self-doubt.

Citrine (pale yellow to orange): *Prosperity, success, positivity, protection.* A form of quartz, citrine is said to get rid of nightmares and boost the spirit. It is associated with the sun, perhaps because of its sunny color, and its name comes from the word "citrus" because of the yellow and orange fruits it resembles.

Crystal quartz (clear): *Power, psychic abilities, healing, protection, magic.* This stone, especially when in the form of a crystal, is associated with the Goddess and the full moon. In magical jewelry it is often combined with silver to honor both. Crystal quartz is used to boost magical and psychic power, and many witches keep one on their altars. Those who do energy healing work often use crystals, especially crystal quartz, to aid in removing blockages and negativity. If you can only have one stone, this is the one to have.

Fluorite (various colors, usually purple, sometimes with blue, green, and clear shading, it also comes in a beautiful rainbow version that combines them all): *Healing, peace, clear thinking, emotional clearing.* Fluorite is not one of the stones that has been historically used with magic, but it is becoming more popular as modern witches discover it. Mainly associated with mental and emotional issues, fluorite can be used to boost mood and reduce stress, aid with clarity, and draw off negativity. I find it very useful as a healing stone since almost all physical issues have mental and emotional components too.

Garnet (deep red): *Protection, healing, energy, strength.* Garnet has traditionally been used for protection, especially against thieves, and to boost energy and endurance. It is also used to boost power during magical work. In healing it is often associated with blood because of its red color, and it is used for issues with the heart or circulatory system. I use it equally for healing and protection work, as well as for magic that involves passion or joy.

Hematite (silvery black): *Grounding, healing, clearing the mind.* An unusually heavy and shiny stone, it is one of my favorites for grounding and focus work. The inside of the stone is often red, so in healing it may be associated with the heart or blood.

....

....

....

....

stones

45

Jade (green to olive green): *Healing, wisdom, love, protection, prosperity, longevity.* Sacred to the Chinese, jade is a powerful stone that is good for almost every magical need. Like other green stones, it is used to attract money and prosperity and boost the garden. In healing it is worn to prevent illness and treat existing issues. Jade is also used in love magic and protection work. Because it is so expensive, some people like to get a small carved piece to carry as a talisman rather than a larger one to put on the altar.

Jasper (various colors): *Protection, healing, and a variety of other uses, depending on the color and type of jasper.* An inexpensive stone that is a form of chalcedony, it makes a good substitute for other pricier rocks. My favorite is red jasper, a brick-red stone that is very protective and also used for healing. Green jasper is used primarily for healing and brown jasper for grounding. I commonly add a small tumbled piece of red jasper to protection charm bags.

Jet (black): *Protection, healing, divination.* Like amber, jet is also not a true stone but is, in fact, fossilized wood that dates back millions of years. Ironically, amber and jet are considered to be the witches' stones, even though they aren't actually rocks. Jet is thought to protect against negativity, psychic attacks, fear, and nightmares. Jet absorbs negativity, which is probably part of why it is used in healing work.

Lapis lazuli (blue, sometimes with flecks of gold pyrite): *Healing, protection, spirituality, psychic ability, love, joy.* Usually just referred to as lapis, this stone was associated with royalty throughout ancient history.

Although its color can vary, the best-quality stones are a vivid royal blue. Lapis is a powerful healing stone on all levels—physical, mental, and spiritual. It is also associated with spirituality in general and spiritual love in particular. Although it can be expensive, it is well worth investing in one special piece.

stones

Inexpensive Substitutions

Some of the gemstones we love may not always be in our budgets. Here are a few less-pricy substitutions you can try for the more expensive stones:

Aventurine → Jade

Citrine → Topaz

Garnet → Ruby

Fluorite (purple) → Amethyst

Herkimer diamond → Diamond

Sodalite → Lapis

....

....

....

....

....

Malachite (green): *Protection, prosperity, love, peace, success in business, power.* Valued by the ancient Egyptians, used by the Greeks to protect children, and thought during the Middle Ages to protect against black magic, malachite has always been one of the stones associated with magical work. It is strongly protective, attracts love, brings peace, and is called "the salesperson's stone" for its ability to draw success to businesses. I have always liked to pair it with lapis for extra power, especially in jewelry, as the Egyptians traditionally did.

Moonstone (white, sometimes blue, pink, or iridescent): *Love, divination, the moon, protection, sleep.* Moonstone, as its name implies, is strongly associated both with the moon and with the Goddess. In bead form it actually resembles a miniature moon and is often worn in jewelry or added to magical wands. Moonstone is said to boost psychic ability, draw in new love, and heal established relationships. It is, I think, a quietly powerful stone that is not as showy as lapis or amethyst but with a gentle power that shouldn't be underestimated.

Onyx (tan, black, white, red, among other colors): *Protection, grounding, healing (especially from grief), focus.* Although it is most commonly thought of as black, much of the black onyx you see today is dyed. This doesn't in any way negate its magical abilities. Black onyx is one of my favorite stones. In fact, my magical name is Onyx. So you can imagine my dismay when I discovered that most black onyx is treated to turn it from its natural banded chalcedony into a solid color. It turns out this has been a tradition since ancient Roman times and that onyx was treasured by the

Egyptians and Greeks as well, so there you go. Black onyx is strongly protective and useful for grounding and increasing focus. If you are doing defensive magic, this is the stone for you. During times of stress, tuck an onyx into your pocket or wear it in a piece of jewelry. You can also find natural onyx carved into small bowls, which are useful for magical work.

Rose quartz (pink): *Love, friendship, peace.* Rose quartz is used for anything to do with the heart, including opening the heart chakra. It is primarily used in love magic, but I like it for its calming properties as well. Who couldn't use a little help in achieving more peace and happiness?

Smoky quartz (light gray): *Grounding, balance, calm, mental and emotional healing.* Smoky quartz is an especially good stone for those dealing with depression or negativity. It can be calming and help to ground you when you are feeling overwhelmed by the world (so most days, if you're like me).

Sodalite (blue, often with white streaks—it looks something like lapis without the gold flecks, although it is rarely as bright): *Healing, peace, relaxation, wisdom, intuition, self-confidence.* Sodalite is primarily used for healing and calming, as well as boosting a spiritual practice. It is strongly associated with the mind, whether to quiet thoughts or increase intuition.

Tiger's eye (brown, with lighter bands): *Courage, protection, prosperity, confidence, luck, energy.* Tiger's eye is associated with the sun and imparts the energy and courage of that star. It can be carried for protection or used in magical work for protection, prosperity, or bravery. If you are going into a frightening or intimidating situation, tiger's eye will help give you the courage to get through it. It is also good for abundance and general good fortune.

stones

Turquoise (blue, blue-green): *Love, friendship, prosperity, healing, protection, luck, courage.* Turquoise is a powerful stone that has been valued in cultures from the ancient Egyptians to many Native American tribes. As you can see by the list above, it can be used for almost any magical task you can think of. Strongly protective and also healing, turquoise is a good stone to place on your altar, if you have one, or wear in a piece of jewelry. It is also used in magical work to attract love or money. Turquoise is also considered to be lucky, which it would be if it brought you love and wealth.

· · · · · · · ·

As with the herbs in the proceeding section, this is just a small sampling of the stones that people use for magic. These are the ones that I find most readily available, easy to work with, and just plain beautiful. If you have others you prefer, feel free to add them here, along with any notes you might have on your work with these or any other stones.

....

....

....

....

....

....

....

....

....

Stones in All Their Forms

Stones come in many different forms, although not all rocks are available in every single one. For instance, there are many gemstones that are naturally formed as crystals, and those may vary from small (to hang off a necklace or tuck in a pocket) to very large showpieces that cost hundreds of dollars. There are also tumbled stones, where the rough rock is put in a machine and tumbled until it is smooth, and those that are left in their rough, chunky form. Many kinds of rocks can be found made into beads or carved into pyramids, hearts, animals, or a myriad of other shapes. (You wouldn't believe how many rocks I have in the shape of cats. Okay, maybe you would.) Which size and shape you buy will depend on what you intend to use it for, what you can find, and, of course, your budget.

stones

stones

54

Stone Sources

Some of us are lucky enough to have stores nearby that carry gemstones and other magical supplies. Others have to go on the internet to find what they need. But back in the day—whatever day that was—witches had to find their stones where they lived.

For some, that might have meant a small shop, a weekly market in the town square, or even a traveling peddler with exotic wares from far away. For others, it would have meant whatever was available in their local area. Agates and quartz are found in Spain, for instance, while some of the best amber is located in Poland. Quartz crystals are abundant in Northern England and Scotland. Early witches most likely would have focused their magical work using the stones that they had easy access to.

Plus there were large stones, either manmade (like Stonehenge) or natural caves and mountains where people might go to connect with the stones' power. Tumbled rocks that were tossed up out of the ocean onto a nearby beach or holey stones that had holes formed by water or erosion were (and are) considered by many to be magical, and they were also known as Odin's stones, faerie stones, hag stones, witch's stones, adder stones, and serpent eggs, among other names.

quartz crystal

stones

56

How to Use Stones

As long as you're not throwing them at people, you can use stones any way you want to. There are, however, some more traditional magical uses that many of us integrate into our Witchcraft practices and everyday lives. Stones, like herbs and other tools, are all part of our efforts to focus our intent and our will. When we use stones that are associated with prosperity, for instance, that is a way of reinforcing our intention to work on that goal.

Because of their innate energy, stones have subtler gifts as well. Just by having them around, we benefit from their particular essence. Here are a few examples of how we can make the most of this earthy energy:

Reinforce the intent of spells and rituals: One of the primary ways that witches use stones and crystals is by using them to help us hone our focus when we are doing spells or rituals to achieve a particular goal. For instance, if you are doing a healing ritual, you may use a piece of lapis or sodalite. For grounding, you might choose hematite or onyx, and to connect with the Goddess on the full moon, you could choose quartz crystal or moonstone. By picking the particular stones that are in tune with your magical work, they can boost the energy you are putting into your spells and rituals.

Charm bags and sachets: Any magical mixture, whether it is tucked into a sachet or a charm bag or placed into a spell box kit, will benefit from the addition of stones that reinforce the energy of all the other ingredients. Whenever I put together a protection charm bag, for instance, I add a small tumbled piece of red jasper.

On the altar: Stones can serve a number of purposes on your altar, whether it is a temporary one put up for a full moon or sabbat ritual or a permanent display that celebrates your witchy practice. Some people use crystals to represent the God and the Goddess. For instance, you might choose a piece of moonstone to symbolize the Goddess and a tiger's eye to honor the God. You can also use stones to stand for the four elements, such as citrine for air, carnelian for fire, turquoise for water, and aventurine for earth.

Boost or change the energy in your home: Whether they are on your altar or placed on shelves or tucked into corners, having stones—especially large or powerful ones—can actually change the energy of the place where you live. I have very large pieces of rose quartz and smoky quartz among my extensive collection of rocks because I feel a particular need for the peace and grounding that they bring. If you want to boost your home's security, you may want to invest in protective stones, and those wishing to draw in prosperity might want to choose stones like jade, aventurine, or malachite. Even if you never do any specific magical work with them, the stones' energy is still there.

Healing work: I do a form of energy healing (kind of like Reiki, it's a more intuitive gift I was given many years ago) and have found over the years that certain stones can be used to aid in healing work. Some draw negative energy out and others produce positive energy and help to unblock stuck places in the body. Certain stones seem to have a special affinity for different parts of the body, and others, such as crystal quartz, are good all-purpose healing tools. If you are interested in nontraditional healing, it might be worth doing some experimentation with various rocks and crystals. Some healers also use particular stones to align with the chakras.

Put it in your pocket: If you need a bit of magic to carry with you, it can be as simple as tucking a tumbled stone or two into your pocket. Giving an important presentation and feeling like you could use a boost in confidence? Carry a piece of carnelian. Going on a first date? It couldn't hurt to bring an amethyst crystal or a small rose quartz. Not only are you carrying that energy with you, but it can be comforting to reach in and touch the smooth, cool stone.

Decoration: Let's not forget that most stones and crystals are just plain beautiful. They are a great way to adorn your home while adding a positive vibe at the same time. Tuck a pretty crystal here and a chunk of rock there and you can celebrate your magic whenever you look at them, whether other folks realize it or not.

....

....

....

....

....

....

....

....

stones

How to Cleanse Stones

- Leave them where the moon can shine on them on the night of the full moon

- Alternately, leave them in the sunlight on a sacred day like Midsummer

- Dip them in a bath of salt and water or hold under running water

- Waft with a sage wand

Note: Before cleansing, double check to make sure that your stone doesn't fade in sunlight or wear away in water.

stones

Candles

My most basic rituals often consist of nothing more than lighting a candle and standing in front of my altar. I might say a spell or simply speak to the Goddess, but the act of lighting that candle helps to shift my consciousness into sacred space.

Candles are one of the most easy to find and simple to use witch's tools. There's no learning curve. If you can light a match, you can use one. You don't need to go to a special store to buy them, although for important magical work you might want to treat yourself to a fancy shape or something that has already been prepared for magical use.

The real bonus to candles is that lots of people have them in their houses. Not everyone has an extensive collection of herbs or a cabinet full of crystals, but there is nothing unusual about a bunch of candles on top of your dresser. For witches who are still in the broom closet, this is one tool you can leave laying around and no one will think twice about it. You can't exactly say that about an athame, can you?

If you are the kind of witch who doesn't have the time or energy to do anything complicated and involved, candles are an easy way to add a magical touch to the simplest Witchcraft. On the other hand, if you like to go that additional step or have a crafty flair, candles lend themselves to all sorts of personal embellishments.

There is something fundamentally powerful about lighting a flame in the dark. It is a symbol of hope, a way of sending out your intentions, and it can be a form of worship in and of itself. On the night of the full moon, I often light a white candle and greet the Goddess, sending her my love and appreciation as the candle flickers on my altar.

A Note on Candle Safety

As witches we love the element of fire, but candles should be handled with care. Always use a firesafe plate or holder, and never leave a candle burning if you aren't going to be in the room. Watch out for pets, too, since they can accidentally burn themselves or knock a candle over if it is within reach.

Different Kinds of Candles

There are a surprising number of options when it comes to using candles.

Beeswax: Made from the honeycomb produced by bees, this is the most natural form of candle and has been used for many centuries. Because bees are sacred to the Goddess and such a vital part of nature, beeswax is an excellent choice for magical work. It smells faintly of honey and burns more slowly than many other types of wax. However, it is also more expensive, so some people save it for special occasions.

Paraffin: The most commonly available type of candle, paraffin is made from petroleum byproducts—not exactly the most Earth-friendly source, but they are affordable and can be found in virtually every color, size, and shape you want. The majority of the candles most witches use are made from paraffin, which is what you usually see in stores.

Soy: Made from soybeans, these candles are becoming more common, although they are usually sold in jars or tubs rather than in freestanding shapes. Another natural option.

Candles also can be made from palm oil, bayberries, and a number of other sources, but these three are the most often used.

candles

Mini lights/chime candles: These mini tapers, bigger than a birthday candle but still quite diminutive, have become very popular for esoteric supplies. They fit well into a magical kit, can be burned down completely for one spell if so desired, and, let's face it, they're cute. I like them because I can have boxes of multiple colors without taking up too much space.

Molded shapes: If you are of a magical inclination, it can be fun to use candles that come in the shape of stars or moons, cats, or Goddess/ female figures and God/male figures, among others. Some of these might be available anywhere, while others would have to be sought out from a New Age or Pagan retailer.

Tapers: Thin and tall, tapers can be simple and inexpensive or fancy and hand-dipped (something you can do at home) or beautifully twisted. Tapers may burn for a longer time and are great to use as God and Goddess candles.

Tealights: Small and flat, tealights are good for fast and simple rituals or times when you want to burn a bunch of candles at the same time. (We use these at Samhain for our ancestor altar so people can light multiple candles for the people they have lost.)

Votives: Votives are a middle size, usually about two inches tall. If you want to use beeswax, this may be a more affordable way to do so. Votives are wider and more squat, and therefore the best option if you wish to etch symbols into your candles before using them.

candles

If you don't have a specific color candle for whatever magical task is at hand, remember you can always substitute white.

....

....

....

....

....

....

....

....

....

....

....

....

....

....

....

....

....

....

....

....

....

....

....

candles

Uses by Color
– a general guide –

In modern Witchcraft, certain colors are often associated with specific magical goals and intentions. This is useful when choosing what candles you are going to use for a particular spell. While these things can vary, and you should always follow whatever your gut says regardless of this kind of list, here is a simple guide to colors to get you started.

Red & Orange: Courage, energy, power, passionate love (red), fire

Pink: Love, calm, self-love, friendship, peace, happiness

Yellow: Intellect and conscious mind, clear speech and communication, creativity, air, the God

Green & Brown: Prosperity and money, success, fertility, growth, luck, healing, earth

Blue: Healing, sleep, calm, purification, water

Purple: Spirit, psychic abilities, purification, meditation

White: The moon, psychic abilities, purification, protection, the Goddess

Black: Protection, power, grounding

Silver: The Goddess

Gold: The God

These colors apply to stones as well as other magical tools, like cloth for charm bags and the like.

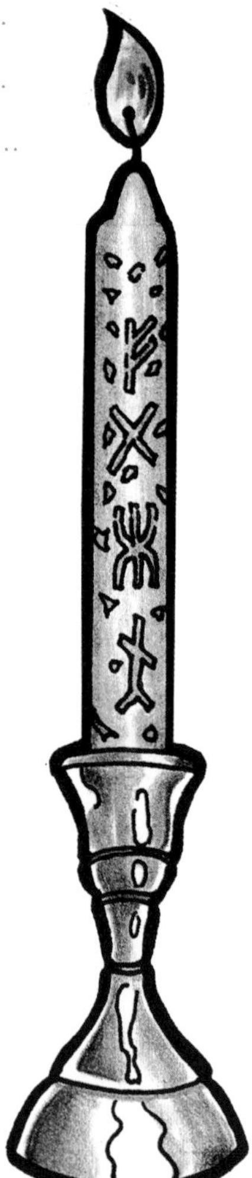

How to Use Candles

This seems like kind of a no-brainer, doesn't it? If you want to use a candle, just lighting the thing is one way to do it. In many rituals, you will simply choose the candle that seems appropriate for the magical work at hand and light it at the time that is right.

For instance, in a formal ritual most witches will light candles to call in each of the four quarters (north, east, south, and west) and one candle each for the God and the Goddess (or sometimes just one for the Goddess, depending on the ritual). They may also light a candle for the specific spellwork they are doing, such as a green candle for a prosperity spell.

There are those, however, who like to take things a step or two beyond the basics. You can, for instance, bless and anoint a candle for magical work, either before or during the ritual in which you intend to use it. Some people also carve symbols into the sides of the candle. If you are doing work for prosperity, those symbols might include rune signs that are associated with wealth and abundance, a dollar sign, your initials, or anything else that has particular meaning for you. For love magic, you would use symbols that are appropriate for that, like hearts, unity symbols, the signs for male or female, or even the word "love."

It is also possible to decorate the outside of the candle in other ways. Say that you are doing protection magic and would have liked to have used a black candle, but all you had was a white one. You can tie a piece of black ribbon or yarn around the bottom (being careful not to let the candle burn down that far) to change the energy. You can also roll the candle in herbs or dried flowers either to boost its magical power or simply to make it more beautiful. Again, just make sure that you are cautious if using anything flammable.

Candles are a surprisingly flexible and potent tool, and their uses are only limited by your imagination. Of course, there is nothing wrong with just lighting a plain white candle, either. Your magic, your choice.

Ritual Candle Basics

4 quarter candles: yellow/east (air),
red/south (fire), blue/west (water),
green/north (earth)

Goddess candle: white or silver

God candle: yellow or gold

Optional: candle for spellwork

candles

Consecrating and Anointing a Candle

If you want to give your ritual candles extra oomph, you can consecrate and anoint them. This can be done ahead of time (either individually or with a number of candles at once) or as a part of whatever ritual you are doing. It can be more convenient to do it ahead of time and have a stockpile of candles ready to go, although doing it during the ritual can help to deepen your focus on the task at hand. Neither way is wrong.

You can use any of the following: magical oil (either purchased or oil you have already created that has a particular purpose, like money-drawing oil, or simply oil for increasing power) or any essential oil that works for the magical task you have in mind, salt, water, a sage wand or incense, a white candle, plus the candle or candles you will be consecrating.

Place everything you will be using on your altar or a table. You may want to spread a cloth under the candles you are working with to catch stray drops of water and bits of salt. Light the white candle and, if you wish, invoke the Goddess and God. Hold up the candle to be consecrated and sprinkle it with a bit of salt, saying, "With the power of earth, I consecrate this candle." Then sprinkle it with some drops of water from the tips of your fingers and say, "With the power of water, I consecrate this candle." Light the sage or incense and waft it over the candle, saying, "With the power of air, I consecrate this candle." (You can also substitute a feather.) Then hold the candle a safe distance over the white candle you lit earlier and say, "With the power of fire, I consecrate this candle."

To anoint the candle, dip your finger into the oil you are using and rub it onto the candle from bottom to top. Be careful not to get any on the wick. Say, "With this magical oil, I anoint this candle and dedicate it to magical work." (If you are using a specific oil, such as one for love, you can say "magical work for love.")

If you wish, you can hold the candle up and say, "I ask the Goddess and God to bless this candle for positive magical work" or simply say, "This candle is now consecrated for magical work. May it do only good and never harm; so mote it be."

Beeswax, Tallow, and Spermaceti, Oh My!

Sometimes it is good to live in the modern age. Witches of old didn't have many of the choices for candles that we have now. Beeswax was available, but unless you happened to keep your own bees, it was very expensive and was only used by the wealthy upper classes. Most candles were made from tallow (rendered animal fat) or spermaceti (whale fat), neither of which burned terribly well or smelled very good. Just another thing to be grateful for as we follow our modern Witchcraft path.

....
....
....
....
....
....
....
....
....
....
....
....
....
....
....
....
....
....
....
....
....
....
....

candles

candles

79

Magical Recipes

primary purpose of a Book of Shadows is to give a witch one place in which to write down all of his or her recipes. By this I don't mean actual cooking recipes, although some folks add in some of those as well, and you'll find a few later on in this book.

The recipes I'm talking about are the magical ones: herbal mixtures, charm bags, and poppet components. After all, it can take a certain amount of trial and error to find the perfect combinations, whether that means what worked for you magically or which combinations are the most pleasant to work with (those that don't stink when you put all the scents together, for example) or are easiest to put together in a hurry. Once you've figured it out, you don't want to start again from scratch the next time, so it makes sense to write it down in your book.

Additionally, some witches share this information, whether with other witches in their coven, if they have one, or an apprentice or family member. In those cases, it is helpful to have the steps written down and gathered in one handy place.

As with any other magical work you do, the recipes in this section are simply a starting point. If you don't like one of the ingredients, feel free to leave it out. If you can't get a component, feel free to substitute something else you think will work or simply do without it. You may want to use the journal pages to make notes about any changes you made or what things worked best for you. You can also add entirely new recipes of your own. You never know when you're going to find someone you wish to share your knowledge with.

Magical recipes may use one tool (such as oils) or a combination of a number of different tools (like herbs, stones, and candles, along with other extras as desired). What they have in common is that each of them is designed to serve a particular purpose. For instance, you might have a magical oil for healing, a healing charm bag, a spell kit that has preassembled all the ingredients you would need for doing healing magic, or a poppet that is intended to channel healing magic for you or someone close to you.

While there are infinite options for magical goals, most of us work toward the same basic ones on a regular basis: healing, prosperity, love, protection, strength, courage, purification, boosting psychic ability or mental clarity, happiness, and peace. These may sometimes be combined, like when we want to work on healing and peace at the same time, because the two issues are connected, but most of the time we are focused on achieving one particular objective.

It can help to have a few recipes already prepared for those issues we are most likely to deal with on a regular basis. That's where this section of your Book of Shadows comes in handy. Of course, there is going to be some overlap if you are working on different approaches to the same problem. If you are putting together both a charm bag and a magical kit for prosperity, for instance, you may find yourself using the same herbs, just in different ways.

Alternately, you can pick whichever approach appeals to you the most, and use that one for all or most of the problems you face. Some people prefer to do simple spells; others make charm bags. With your collection of recipes, you have a few options to choose from.

....

....

....

....

....

....

....

....

....

....

....

....

....

....

....

magical recipes

Magical Oils

These are my favorite combinations, arrived at after years of experimentation. You may want to refer back to the section on herbs and do your own experimenting to see if there are other pairings you like better. These are all created using essential oils, which carry a strong energy from the original plant. Remember that fragrance oils will not have the same power since they are artificial.

You can usually find essential oils at health food stores, sometimes even in the health food section of regular grocery stores if you are looking for common ones. You can also find them readily available online and at some Pagan and New Age shops. If you don't want to invest in dozens of different oils, you may want to see which ones you would use the most and start with them. For instance, lavender and peppermint have multiple uses, both magical and medicinal. If you get food-grade oils, you can even use them in cooking.

Some essential oils, like chamomile and rose, are considerably more expensive than others. But a little bit goes a long way, so you can buy a tiny bottle and only use one or two drops. You can also substitute something else less pricy—it is up to you.

To create a magical oil, you will need a base oil. There are many different options, such as almond, safflower, grapeseed, and jojoba. I use olive oil from my kitchen rather than buying something special, but keep in mind that it may go rancid faster than the other options, so you will want to make smaller batches if you use it.

You should store your magical oil in a dark-colored glass container. I like the cobalt blue bottles, but you can also get brown or other shades. Clear glass lets in light, and that will cause the oils to degrade faster. Pour in your base oil and then add a few drops of each essential oil you are using. I like to use a total of nine drops because nine is a magical number, but you can use more if you want the scent to be stronger. Remember to focus on your goal with each drop you add, and then when you are finished, swirl the oil gently in a clockwise direction to blend it all together. Store it out of direct sunlight.

Magical oils can be used to anoint candles, crystals, amulets, or charm bags. They can also be used to anoint those taking part in a ritual if you have used skin-safe essential oils. (All of those listed here should be fine as long as you aren't allergic to them.)

Energy/Strength/Courage: cinnamon (3 drops), ginger (3 drops), lemon or orange (3 drops)

Healing: lavender (4 drops), lemon balm (2 drops), rosemary (3 drops)

Lemon balm can be more expensive and harder to find, although I really like it. You can substitute eucalyptus if you prefer.

Love: rose geranium (3 drops), lavender (3 drops), rose (3 drops)

Rose is another expensive one, although it is very powerful. You can substitute lemon or, if you are looking for passionate love, use cinnamon.

Peace & Happiness: chamomile (2 drops), rose geranium (4 drops), lavender (3 drops)

If you don't have chamomile, you can use an extra drop of the other two or else use lemon instead. Lemon balm is also a good addition if you have it.

Prosperity: basil (2 drops), cinnamon (3 drops), peppermint (4 drops)

Protection: rosemary (4 drops), basil (2 drops), sage (3 drops)

Purification: rosemary (2 drops), sage (2 drops), lemon (3 drops), lavender (2 drops)

Note that there is a lot of crossover in the ingredients for protection and purification, so you could easily make a combo oil that works for both.

magical recipes

Warning

There is some evidence that using essential oils in diffusers can be dangerous, possibly even fatal, to pets, so if you have pets, you might want to exercise extra caution with your magical oils. Essential oils are very concentrated, so a tiny amount can cause issues even if your pet doesn't come into direct contact and even if the ingredients would be safe in normal usage.

Charm Bags

Charm bags are a way to put the ingredients for a spell into a bag that can then be hung up in your home, tucked under your pillow, placed on your altar, or given as a gift. You can also take the same basic ingredients and make them into a sachet or small pillow. The only difference between charm bags and sachets is that the first one opens and the second is sewn shut.

Charm bags are easy to make. For one thing, you can simply buy a premade drawstring bag made of anything from silk to cotton to velvet to leather in whatever size suits your needs. If you are into making your own, you can sew one or simply use a square of cloth and tie it up with a ribbon or piece of yarn.

The choice of bag or cloth is up to you. Some witches like to use only natural fabrics, such as silk or cotton, while others use whatever they have on hand. It can be nice to use a fabric whose color matches your magical intention—like blue for healing—but white or plain undyed muslin lend themselves to any goal, and you can then draw symbols on the cloth if you want to.

There is no right way to do this. Whatever works for you is fine. Sometimes I use a square of cloth and sometimes I choose from my (admittedly large) collection of drawstring bags. It mostly depends on what I'm in the mood for or which is easiest to find when it is time to do the magical work.

Easy Protection Charm Bag

Place a piece of red jasper or black onyx in the middle of a 3 x 3-inch square of white cloth. Add some dried rosemary, a garlic clove, some dried basil, and a couple pinches of sea salt. As you tie the cloth shut around the contents with a ribbon, focus on your intent to protect your home. Hang it near your house's main entrance.

Once you have chosen your bag, you need to decide what you are going to put inside it. Chose any of the following that fit with your magical goal: herbs, tumbled stones or crystals, charms or amulets, or any other items that feel appropriate. For instance, if you are creating a prosperity-drawing bag, you may want to put a shiny penny or a half dollar in it to represent money. For protection bags, it was traditional to put in a pin. I think it was supposed to impale evil or something to that effect—just make sure you don't impale yourself by accident!

Assemble all your ingredients and the bag or cloth and lay them out on your altar or on a flat surface like a table or the floor (or the ground, if you are working outside). If you are using a spell, you may want to write down a copy of it on a small piece of paper and roll it up to tuck inside, or you could write the name of your goal on a piece of paper instead and/or include some symbols that represent it.

Make sure that as you add each item, you concentrate on your magical goal. When you're done, either pull the drawstring tight or tie the ribbon around the top of the cloth bundle, making it into a bag. If you want a little extra oomph, you can anoint your charm bag with magical oil.

If you so desire, you can take it one extra step and bless and consecrate it; if not, simply hang or place it wherever you intend to keep it. Protection charm bags are often hung over the entrance door to your home, although you can also place one in your child's room or in your car. If you can't leave them out where they might be seen, you can always tuck them in the back of a drawer or in your glove compartment. It is also possible to make very small ones, usually called amulets, and hang them from a cord around your neck.

Note that in the following recipes, it is generally better to use dried herbs since the fresh ones probably won't last as long. Fresh rose petals are lovely, for instance, but they contain more moisture, so they will eventually get moldy. You can use fresh herbs if you are only planning on having the charm bag around for a short time, like a week or two.

You can also pick and choose from all the various items listed; you don't have to use them all. In part it will depend on what you have on hand or can get easily and what your gut tells you to use. Usually I use three or four different kinds of herbs and one tumbled stone or small crystal plus either a written spell or some kind of token to symbolize my intent.

Energy/Strength/Courage. *Herbs:* sticks of cinnamon, dried ginger, dried orange or lemon peel, thyme. *Stones:* carnelian, agate, amber, garnet, tiger's eye, turquoise. *Symbols:* the rune stone Uraz, the sun, an ox or bull. *Colors:* red or orange.

Healing. *Herbs:* lavender, lemon balm, rosemary, calendula, eucalyptus, cinnamon, garlic, mint, thyme. *Stones:* crystal quartz, amethyst, carnelian, garnet, lapis, turquoise, sodalite, fluorite, hematite, jade, jet. *Symbols:* the caduceus (the staff with snakes entwined around it that stands for healing), a sun with a spiral inside, the lotus, the rune stones Uraz, Kenaz, Sigel, Tir, or Ing. *Color:* blue.

Love. *Herbs:* lavender, rose petals, carnation, lemon peel, cinnamon (for passionate love). *Stones:* amethyst, rose quartz, turquoise, garnet, amber, jade, lapis, malachite, moonstone. *Symbols:* hearts, clasped hands, a circle, the rune stones Fehu, Kenaz, Gifu, Wunjo, Beorc, or Ing. *Colors:* pink (romantic love, family love) or red (passionate love). You can use a stone in the shape of a heart and it will do double duty.

Peace & Happiness. *Herbs:* chamomile, lavender, rose geranium, rose petals, catnip, lemon balm. *Stones:* amethyst, lapis, sodalite, blue lace agate, crystal quartz, fluorite, rose quartz, malachite, smoky quartz. *Symbols:* Heart, dove, peace sign, laughing Buddha, the rune Wunjo. *Color:* blue.

Prosperity. *Herbs:* basil, cinnamon, peppermint, ginger, dill, chamomile. *Stones:* aventurine, green quartz, malachite, tiger's eye, jade, turquoise, citrine. *Symbols:* coins (actual coins or pictures), a four-leaf clover, an acorn, the rune stones Fehu, Daeg, Othel, Gifu, Uraz, or Tir. *Colors:* green or gold.

Protection. *Herbs:* rosemary, basil, sage, garlic, dill, parsley. *Stones:* Black onyx, agate, red jasper, amber, crystal quartz, tiger's eye, garnet, carnelian, amethyst, turquoise, jade, lapis, moonstone, jet. *Symbols:* shield, pentacle/pentagram, the Eye of Ra (Egyptian), the rune stones Thurisaz, Eihwaz, Eolh, or Kenaz. *Colors:* black or white.

• • • • • • • • •

These are the basics, but you can create a charm bag for virtually any need. Just put together some of the herbs and a stone from the earlier sections of this book, and use a symbol or a spell that has meaning to you.

A Charm Bag for Prosperity

Take a green bag or cloth and put inside a small amount of basil, a cinnamon stick, and some peppermint leaves. (If you don't have peppermint leaves in your kitchen or magical supplies, you can use a peppermint tea bag.) Add a piece of aventurine (or any other green stone) and a coin. If you are using a penny, make sure it is bright and shiny, or else use a dollar or half dollar coin or even some play money. Write the following spell down on a slip of paper and tuck it inside the bag: "God and Goddess, hear my plea: rain prosperity down on me. Bring in monies large and small to pay my bills, one and all. Money earned and gifts for free—as I will, so mote it be." As you place each item inside, concentrate on your desire for prosperity in any positive form. Tie the bag shut and put it somewhere safe.

Poppets

In essence, a poppet is a magical doll—but not the kind you play with. Poppets are, in fact, very serious magic, and their use can be found—in one form or another—in many cultures going back to early times. Poppets can be made out of various different materials, including clay, wax, dough, and wood, but most often they are crafted out of fabric.

A poppet is a representation of a person, either someone else or yourself, and by doing magical work on the poppet through the use of sympathetic magic, you can affect the person that doll represents. Obviously, this can be used for things like hexing (causing ill), but I strongly recommend against that as such things have a way of coming back to bite you. Just sayin'.

But you can make a poppet to send healing energy to a friend—with their permission—or work magic for yourself.

Start crafting the doll by cutting out the basic outline of a human being from cloth: arms, legs, torso, head. Think of a gingerbread man. You will want two pieces so you can sew them together. Don't worry if your sewing skills aren't great; this isn't meant to be a work of art, just a practical object. (And there is always glue if you are desperate, although the act of sewing allows you to put your intent into the poppet with every stitch.)

You will want to have something about the poppet that shows who it is supposed to represent. You could use black yarn to stand for dark hair, for instance. Some people will use something called a "taglock." This is an item that ties the poppet to the person it stands for. It could be a strand of hair or a fingernail clipping, an item that belongs to the person, or even the person's name written down on a piece of paper. This all sounds kind of creepy, doesn't it? It doesn't have to be, especially if you are doing work for yourself, but I like to simply make the doll look a bit like the person it is for or write their initials on the back.

Sew the doll about three quarters of the way. Finish the arms, torso, and legs or else start midway down one side and go almost all the way around so you can start stuffing the dolly with cotton batting, tissue, or even straw. You may want to include some herbs that are associated with your magical intention, and tuck your taglock inside if you are using one. You can even write a spell or a word on a piece of paper (like "healing" or "draw in love" or "protection") and roll it up inside the middle of the doll. Once you have done that, finish sewing it up, leaving a tiny spot open to allow you to stuff the head, then close that up too.

You may want to bless and consecrate your poppet, and either put it on your altar or hide it away, depending on its purpose and your living situation.

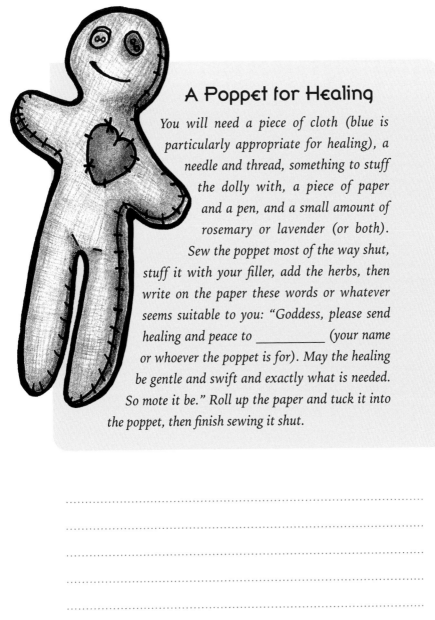

A Poppet for Healing

You will need a piece of cloth (blue is particularly appropriate for healing), a needle and thread, something to stuff the dolly with, a piece of paper and a pen, and a small amount of rosemary or lavender (or both). Sew the poppet most of the way shut, stuff it with your filler, add the herbs, then write on the paper these words or whatever seems suitable to you: "Goddess, please send healing and peace to _____ (your name or whoever the poppet is for). May the healing be gentle and swift and exactly what is needed. So mote it be." Roll up the paper and tuck it into the poppet, then finish sewing it shut.

Divination

*T*here are many different forms of divination. Some witches don't use any of them and others use them all. Most of us, though, discover over time and through experimentation the ones that work best for us. Divination is a way of tapping into our own inner wisdom and/or guidance from the universe, the gods, or our personal guides. There are a number of tools that can help us do this, but none of them work if you don't approach the task with a serious attitude and a certain faith in your own ability to listen to those messages you receive.

That doesn't mean divination can't be fun or that you have to be blessed with an unusual talent to make it work. As with everything else, some people have an innate gift for divination, but with practice and patience, it is something almost everyone can do.

Tarot Cards

Tarot cards are one of the most well known and commonly used forms of divination. They come in an incredibly diverse range of images and themes, so there should be a deck that appeals to almost everyone. It might, however, take a certain amount of trial and error to discover which one (or ones) suits you best. Some people collect dozens of decks and others find one favorite and stick with that forever. Either way is just fine.

Don't be discouraged if reading tarot cards doesn't work for you right away. This is definitely an area of Witchcraft where practice makes perfect, or at least more comfortable. Some people have a gift for it and others have to find their way over time. Another thing to keep in mind is that not everyone is equally good at reading for themselves and reading for others; often it is one or the other. I have been reading tarot professionally for over twenty years, yet I can't do a reading for myself with any degree of accuracy. On the other hand, I have friends who can read for themselves but not for others.

The most commonly used decks are some variation on the basic Rider-Waite version. Like most others, this deck has seventy-eight cards, made up of the major arcana and the minor arcana. Some people find the symbolism of this older-style deck difficult to understand, but if that is true for you, there are plenty of more modern alternatives.

It might be helpful to think of the cards as a tool that helps you channel your own inner wisdom or guidance from outside, rather than a rigid guideline. While the card descriptions that come with many of the decks can be helpful when you are first starting out, eventually you may not need to follow them as closely once your own intuition takes over.

Oracle Cards

For those that find the tarot too confusing or just don't resonate with it, oracle cards can be a simpler alternative. Like the tarot, oracle cards come in an almost infinite variety. Some decks have as few as twenty-four cards, some as many as eighty, but usually they are smaller decks and much less complicated. The cards usually have a basic, easy-to-understand message, so there is less interpretation needed.

Oracle cards are usually used individually rather than in spreads (groupings of multiple cards, which are often used in tarot readings), which can make using them a little easier. Like tarot cards, oracle cards can be used both for serious divination and for fun, as well as for guidance and answers to questions.

My Favorite Decks

I admit to being somewhat prejudiced when it comes to my favorite decks since I have had the amazing good fortune to be able to design my own and work with the fabulous illustrator Elisabeth Alba to create both the Everyday Witch Tarot deck and the Everyday Witch Oracle. However, before I had my own decks to use, my go-to deck for doing readings was the classic Universal Waite deck with illustrations by Pamela Colman Smith, recolored by Mary Hanson-Roberts.

Rune Stones

Rune stones are a form of ancient language or symbolism. The most commonly used are the Norse/Germanic runes called the Elder Futhark, which can vary somewhat in how they are spelled and the way they are drawn. There are twenty-four stones in a set (three sets of eight), usually along with a blank called the Wyrd, which may symbolize either the unknowable or open possibilities.

Despite the fact that they are often referred to as rune stones, the earliest rune sets were made out of wood, and it is still possible to find or make a set on simple wooden rounds. More often, though, we see them made out of either polished stone or clay, with the rune symbols either etched or drawn on. They are usually kept in some kind of bag or pouch, although a nice wooden box will work well too.

Rune stones can be fairly easy to use, in part because there is less interpretation needed than with something like tarot. You might pull out one rune to answer a simple question or pull three for a "past, present, future" reading. Say, for instance, that you want to know whether or not you should take a particular trip. If you pull out Raidho, which means travel or movement, the answer is probably yes. On the other hand, if you end up with Isa, which symbolizes delay or lack of action, it either means that you should wait or if you do take the trip, you should probably prepare yourself for some delays along the way.

One good way to acquaint yourself with the runes is to take a month and practice pulling one out every day. It is an interesting exercise in which you can see how often the rune you get does, in fact, have some connection to the events of the day, and it helps you become familiar with the runes themselves. The high priestess who led the first group I belonged to had us do this, and it was both fun and helpful. You can use the journal pages in this section to record the runes you pull and whether or not they were accurate.

Making Your Own Runes

It is surprisingly easy to make your own set of rune stones. If you are at all handy with tools and have the right equipment, you can use a piece of wood that is around ¾″ in diameter and slice it into 25 pieces. (You can use a branch if you can find one the right size or buy a finished piece of wood.) Then either use a wood-burning tool or a pen to draw the runes on one side. Alternately, you can find 25 flattish stones of around the same size and shape—either from the beach or in your yard or purchased at a gardening or aquarium supply store—and paint or draw the runes on those. I once made a set from clay, which a group member who was a potter fired for us, but you can also use the kind of clay that doesn't need to be fired or that is finished in the oven. Rune stones you made yourself may not be as pretty as ones you buy, but they will be imbued with your own energy, which is a definite advantage when it comes to using them for divination.

Scrying

For an extremely simple (although not necessarily easy) type of divination, you can try one form or another of scrying, which is a method of divination where you look into something for messages. The classic image of a witch with a crystal ball is one example, although most of us can't afford a crystal that large. More often, modern witches use either a scrying mirror, which is either made of black glass, clear glass that has been painted black on one side, or a shallow dark bowl filled with water. You can peer into these under the light of a full moon or by candlelight and see if you can see images forming in the otherwise blank space. Reading tea leaves is another type of scrying, in which tea is made with loose leaves; once the liquid has been consumed, the future is read in the leaves remaining on the bottom of the cup.

Scrying involves concentration and the ability to empty your mind of conscious thought so that the unconscious mind is open to whatever messages come through. I confess, I have never had much luck with scrying, despite my ease with using tarot and oracle cards and rune stones. Not everyone is good at every kind of divination, and scrying doesn't seem to be one of my gifts, but perhaps it is yours.

divination

Pendulums

Pendulums are probably the simplest of all forms of divination—so simple, in fact, that they are primarily most useful for yes and no answers. Still, there are plenty of times when that is all you need, and pendulums are inexpensive, easy to store, and often very pretty.

A pendulum is usually a chain or string with something hanging from the end. That "something" can vary greatly, although witches are often partial to gemstones like amethyst and crystal quartz.

Magical pendulums are very easy to use. First you have to set, or calibrate, it so that you know how exactly your pendulum gives you three main answers: yes, no, or uncertain/maybe. For instance, some pendulums answer yes by swinging from left to right, and others by turning in a circle. The first time you use a new pendulum, you will want to either ask it to "Say yes," or ask it a question for which you know the answer is yes, like "Is my name _____?" (I'm aware that I'm telling you to talk to an inanimate object, but really, I promise this works and isn't as odd as it sounds. Well, maybe it *is* as odd as it sounds, but it still works.)

Once you have figured out how the pendulum gives you a yes answer, repeat the same thing by asking it to say no or by asking it a question to which the answer is no, like "Am I standing on the moon?" The indefinite answer will be anything other than those two things.

Most pendulums either do left to right or clockwise for yes and right to left or counterclockwise for no, but you will need to check yours to find out. Once the tool is set for you, you can use it not only for simple yes and no questions but also to help you make choices between multiple options (you can write them on a piece of paper and see which way the pendulum swings) or, in theory, even for dowsing (finding things).

A Simple Paperclip Pendulum

You can make a cheap and easy version of a pendulum by simply hanging a paperclip from a piece of string or thick thread. It should work just as well as the fancy ones, although it won't be as pretty.

Dream Divination

The technical word for dream divination is oneiromancy. Don't worry—you don't have to be able to pronounce it to do it. Dream divination is a way of inviting the answers to your questions to show up while you are sleeping. At its most basic, you simply think of the question you need answered right before you fall asleep. This invites your subconscious to work on the problem, as well as opening your psyche to information from outside your own mind.

For a more magical approach, you might petition gods and goddesses who are associated with sleep and dreaming. Morpheus, for example, is the Greek god of dreams. Hypnos, from whom we get the word hypnosis, is also a god of sleep. The Celtic horse goddess Epona is also associated with dreaming.

You can also just reach out to deity in general or your own personal gods and ask them to send you clarity and direction. Mind you, they may not wait for you to ask. If you have dreams that are unusually vivid and meaningful, the universe may be sending you messages on its own. It is up to you to be paying attention.

Not all dreams are portents of the future. In fact, most of them are usually the fanciful ramblings of our own brains. How can you tell the difference? Sometimes you can't. That's why some people keep dream journals and write down whatever dreams they can remember right after they wake up in the morning. If the same symbols or people show up repeatedly, it might be worth taking a closer look at those dreams. Remember that things in dreams are not always what they seem. For instance, if you dream of a snake going underground, that might mean a time of transition and change, whereas a poisonous snake might warn of betrayal.

If you intend to do purposeful dream divination, it might be helpful to prepare yourself with a magical cleansing bath or a short period of meditation before going to bed. Clear your mind as best you can and focus on what it is you wish to dream about. For an added boost, you can try tucking a dream charm bag under your pillow before you go to sleep.

....

....

....

....

....

....

A Dream Charm Bag

You can either use a small drawstring bag of some kind or create a sachet by sewing up three sides of a piece of cloth, filling it, and then sewing up the final edge to create a tiny pillow. The herb most commonly used for dream work is mugwort, but you can also use lavender, rosemary, chamomile, lemon balm, hops, and even catnip (although if your cat sleeps with you, you might end up fighting to keep your charm bag to yourself). Some people like to place a gemstone inside as well; amethyst, lapis, or crystal quartz are good ones to use. Place the herbs, and stone if using, inside the bag and then tuck it under your pillow before going to sleep.

divination

....
....
....
....
....
....
....
....
....
....
....
....
....
....
....
....
....
....
....
....
....

* To do: make my own set of
Ogham symbols!

divination

Gods and Goddesses

Undoubtedly the most personal aspect of a Witchcraft practice centers around the worship of the God and Goddess. Or sometimes only a specific goddess, depending on the witch. Or oftentimes more than one god and goddess. When it comes down to it, the choice of which candle colors or herbs you use for a spell are much less important than where you place your faith.

A witch's Book of Shadows may be used to document the exploration of different pantheons or research into various deities. It might be a place where you make a note of symbols and signs that appear to you (whether in day-to-day life or in dreams) that might signify a connection with one particular god or goddess. Or it could hold a record of interactions with deity, invocations used to call on the God and the Goddess, and so much more.

You can use the journal pages in this section for these purposes or anything else that seems right to you.

Some witches follow a particular pantheon (deities who come from the same culture). Others worship a variety of different deities, depending on which ones they feel a connection to. It isn't actually necessary to pick a specific deity. Some folks simply call on "God and Goddess" in a general way, and that is just fine. In my case, I often invoke a nonspecific God and Goddess, and occasionally call on someone in particular when it feels right to do so.

If you have already been practicing Witchcraft for some time, you probably know the answers to these questions already. But if you are just starting out or if you feel as though your practice needs to change and grow, figuring out which gods interest you the most can be a good place to start. There are a couple of different ways to go about this. You can look at the gods by pantheon (the cultures they come from) and/or which particular traits they are most strongly associated with, or you can try to figure out where in your life you most need help from a force greater than yourself. You may want to follow gods from a pantheon related to the culture you were born into, for instance, or one which you feel called to. This may change over time and practice, too.

Listening When They Speak

Sometimes you have to go looking for the god or goddess you are meant to worship. Sometimes, though, they come looking for you. They may send you repeated signs and symbols or show up in your dreams or when you meditate. These messages can be easy to miss unless you are paying attention. Be quiet and listen for a voice that comes from outside of you.

Gods and Goddesses by Attributes

One way to look for a deity who resonates with you is to find one with the attributes that appeal to you or fill a need. At various different times in our lives, we may be drawn to gods who are associated with love or abundance or strength or wisdom. Most gods and goddesses have more than one attribute; ironically, many goddesses of love are also goddesses of war. (Okay, maybe that's not so far-fetched. Relationships are tough.)

However, just like people, deities are more than just the sum of their parts. They are complicated and multifaceted. It isn't enough to just say, "Okay, this says Eros is a god of love; I'll follow him." Eros is primarily associated with young love, sexual desire, and passion. If you are actually looking for a god to help you with mature, steady, romantic love, you should probably look elsewhere.

But since we want our Book of Shadows to be a handy reference guide to the practice of Witchcraft, to give you a place to start, here is a simple breakdown of some of the attributes you might be looking for.

Love

Need to whip up a spell to draw love to your life, encourage love, reignite a spark, or smooth things over with a loved one? Here are some deities that have love associations you should look into:

- Aengus
- Aphrodite
- Astarte
- Bastet
- Cupid

- Eros

- Freya

- Hathor

- Inanna

- Ishtar

- Isis

Wisdom/Knowledge

Who couldn't use a little more wisdom? If you are in search of knowledge or the best path to expanding your horizons, try checking out one of these deities for guidance:

- Athena

- Cerridwen

- Minerva

Dawn/Youth/Spring

Need a new start or some youthful exuberance? Want to celebrate spring with an appropriate god or goddess? Here are a few that you can look into first:

- Eos

- Eostre

- Flora

- Idun

- Persephone

Prophecy

Seeking answers or want to peer into the future? Back away from that Ouija board and look into these prophetic deities instead:

- Apollo
- Brigit
- Ceridwen
- Morrigan

Healing/Peace/Rest

Hands up, everyone who needs more healing, rest, or peace (raises hand). These deities may be just who you are looking for to aid you in your quest:

- Apollo
- Belenus
- Brigit
- Eir
- Isis
- Kuan Yin
- Morpheus
- Nuada
- Rhiannon

....

....

....

....

....

The Elements

To connect with the elements, or aspects of the planet we live on and with, try checking out one or more of these gods and goddesses. Tread carefully, though, since the elemental gods can sometimes be a little volatile!

- Aegir (sea)
- Apollo (sun)
- Cailleach (storms)
- Gaia (earth)
- Jupiter (skies, thunder)
- Lugh (sun)
- Njord (sea, winds)
- Nox (night)
- Nut (sky)
- Poseidon (sea)
- Ra (sun)
- Thor (thunder, storms)
- Zeus (sky, thunder)

Home & Hearth

Our homes are where our hearts are, so if you want to work on protecting yours or set up an altar that demonstrates that focus, you might consider checking out one of these goddesses:

- Brigit
- Hera
- Hestia
- Holle
- Vesta

Animals/The Wild Lands

For many of us, a Pagan practice brings with it a connection to the land and the animals who live on it. If you want to connect with a deity that shares that connection, one of these might be just who you are looking for:

- Artemis
- Bastet
- Cernunnos
- Cybele
- Diana
- Faunus
- Herne
- Pan

Childbirth/Motherhood

The Goddess is mother to us all in most of her forms, but these deities in particular can be called upon for issues to do with childbirth or motherhood:

- Artemis
- Bes
- Ceres
- Demeter

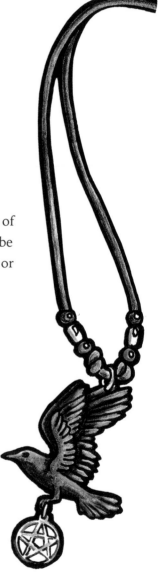

Prosperity/Luck/Abundance

If prosperity, abundance, and luck are what you are looking for, fortune might favor those who make a connection with these deities. Just remember to ask nicely!

- Ceres
- Demeter
- Fortuna
- Freya
- Proserpina
- Saturn
- The Dagda/Daghda

Crafts/Creativity

If you need a hand with your crafty or creative endeavors, these deities have long associations with those who create in various different ways:

- Apollo
- Bragi
- Brigit
- Ceridwen
- Hephaestus
- Hermes
- Lugh
- Minerva
- Vulcan

Protection

Protection work is one of the classic uses of Witchcraft. If you need to ask a god or goddess for help keeping yourself or loved ones safe, you might want to try one of these deities:

- Bastet
- Bes
- Heimdall
- Isis
- Sekhmet
- Thor

• • • • • • • •

Again, this is the most basic of lists. Most of the gods and goddesses associated with the harvest and growth, for instance, are also worshipped for prosperity, since those two things were tied so closely together for our Pagan ancestors. And if you are looking for a deity to worship on a regular basis rather than to call on for a particular temporary need, you will want to find one whose entire essence resonates with you, rather than just one particular trait.

Patrons & Matrons

You sometimes see a deity referred to as
"the patron god of thieves" or "the matron
goddess of weavers." Some witches have
deities they consider to be their own personal
patron/matron deities. Sometimes you choose
them. Sometimes they choose you. Either way, you
may end up having one main deity you worship, even
if you sometimes call on others for help in particular
areas or on specific occasions. Hecate has been mine
for years. I rarely call on her by name, but when I
envision a goddess, she is often who I see hov-
ering over me. If you have a patron deity, you
might dedicate an altar to them, place their
symbols around your home, or put out
offerings to them on important days.

Moon Goddesses & Goddesses of Witches

While it is true that each of us is drawn to our own deities (if, in fact, we are called by specific gods and goddesses at all), it is also true that in modern Witchcraft there are a few goddesses who tend to be particularly revered because of their association with witches, magic, and the moon.

So if you need a place to start, you might want to begin with these particularly magical goddesses:

Witches/Magic: Diana, Freya, Hecate, Isis

Moon: Arianrhod, Artemis, Cerridwin, Diana, Hecate, Luna, Selene (note that the god Thoth is also associated with the moon)

Lunar goddesses are worshipped in conjunction with the moon, so you might call on them during the full moon or, in the case of Hecate, the dark moon. The goddesses who are associated with Witchcraft can be called upon during any magical work or simply for encouragement, protection, or empowerment.

Invocations and Quarter Calls

Whether you are doing a simple solitary ritual in your backyard under a full moon or holding a major sabbat gathering with thirty people, you will probably want to have some basic quarter calls and God/dess invocations in your Book of Shadows.

Keep in mind that not all occasions call for the formality of such things, and some witches never use them at all. But for those who are just starting out or those who work in a group or even people who simply like the rhythm and grace of this part of a ritual, it is handy to have a variety on hand for different occasions.

Invocations

An invocation is a way of calling on God or Goddess. This should always be done with respect, as it is an invitation for them to join you in ritual, not a demand. Usually we light a candle as we invoke the gods, but there is no rule that says you have to. If you are going to use candles, white is always appropriate, or you can use gold or yellow for the God and silver or white for the Goddess. If a particular color is associated with a deity (such as black for Hecate or green for any of the forest/nature gods), you can use that instead.

There are basic invocations that can be used with any deity for any purpose, and there are those that are specific to particular gods or occasions. A Book of Shadows might include some of the more general type, and then ones that a witch has written for his or her patron deity or for sabbat rituals that call on certain deities, and so on.

Blue Moon Circle's Book of Shadows contains copies of all the rituals we have done over the years, including the invocations and quarter calls we used in them. Some invocations might only be used once, and others that are more general may be utilized over and over again. When I am putting together a ritual at the last minute or when I'm tired, it is a huge help to have these already written and ready to use.

If you don't want or need to call on a specific god or goddess, you can use a general invocation. For instance, you might light a candle on the full moon and say, "Great Goddess, I come before you on this, your night of the full moon, and ask that you lend me your strength and your blessing." (Note that on the full moon, we tend to call on Goddess and not God.)

See? Simple but still very effective. For specific deities, you would invoke them by name, possibly using their titles or mentioning aspects that are associated with them: "Hail Thor, God of Thunder, Lord of Lightning," for example. You see what I mean. On a sabbat like Imbolc or Samhain, if you are not calling on a god and a goddess in general, you would probably invoke deities who are linked to those holidays, like Brigid at Imbolc or Hecate at Samhain. You can also invoke your own personal deity, if you have one, on all these occasions.

Here are some examples, but feel free to add any of your own in the journal spaces.

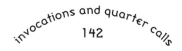

General Invocations

Great Goddess, great God,
please join me in my magical rite and
watch over me as I work this night.

God and Goddess bright and wise,
come to me and help me work my magic.
Guide my words and my actions and
lend me your aid. So mote it be.

Full Moon Goddess Invocations for Solitaries

Great Goddess, lady of the shining moon and the shifting tides, I call your name. On this night of power, I come before you to practice my Craft. Shine your light upon my circle cast with love and lend me your strength and grace. Welcome and blessed be.

Greetings, O Shining One. I, your daughter/son, call upon you this night and ask that you bless me with your presence. Come to me, Mother of All! Come be with me!

A Group Full Moon Invocation

Great Lady, we have gathered together to work our magic in your name. In perfect love and perfect trust, we have come together as one. In perfect love and perfect trust, we ask you to join us. So mote it be!

New Moon/Dark Moon
Goddess Invocation

Great Goddess, in the darkness amid the quiet spaces,
I call to you! Come to me on this night and fill the silence
with your wisdom and my magic with your power. Honor
me with your presence. Welcome and blessed be.

Multiple Goddess Invocation

This can also be done by chanting the goddesses' names since this is a commonly used chant.

Isis, Astarte, Diana, Hecate, Demeter, Kali, Inanna!
Isis, Astarte, Diana, Hecate, Demeter, Kali, Inanna!
My goddesses, I call on you!
My goddesses, hear me!
My goddesses, be with me!
Isis, Astarte, Diana, Hecate, Demeter, Kali, Inanna!

God and Goddess Invocations for the Sabbats

Imbolc

(General) *Great Goddess who causes the earth to stir and begin to awaken, I greet you and welcome you to my Imbolc rite. Great God who wakes the animals and brings back the sun, I welcome you to my Imbolc rite. Welcome and blessed be.*

(Specific) *Blessed Brigid, goddess of smithcraft, poetry, and healing, I invoke you. You who are the fire of creation, the light in the darkness, and warmth during the cold, I call you and welcome you into my circle.*

Great Herne, lord of the animals, protector of the wood, keeper of the dark places. You who remind us that there is always light in the darkness, I call you and welcome you to my circle.

Spring Equinox

(General) *Great Goddess, great God, you have freed yourself from the icy prison of winter. Now is the greening of the world. Life renews itself by your magic, Earth Goddess. The God stretches and rises, eager in his youth and burning with the promise of warmer days to come. Join me here today and gift me with the touch of your energy.*

(Specific) *I invoke Eostre, goddess of the spring. May you join me in my circle and help me to embrace the energy and rebirth that come with this new season. Welcome and blessed be!*

I invoke Zephyrus, god of the west winds, who from days of old has announced the arrival of spring by blowing in the warmer air and fresh ideas. Welcome and blessed be!

....

....

....

....

....

....

....

....

(General) *Great Goddess who makes the fields grow and the flowers bloom, and whose love encompasses us all, I call upon you to bring your joy and beauty to my ritual in celebration of Beltane.*

Great God, lord of the sun who shines bright upon the earth, I call upon you to bring your energy and vitality to my ritual in celebration of Beltane.

(Specific) *Beautiful Aphrodite, embodiment of love and passion, join me on this day of joyous celebration and bless me with your bright and shining spirit. So mote it be.*

Great Pan, lord of the woods and king of the wild creatures, join me on this day of joyous celebration and bless me with the gifts of connection to the world and a spark of carefree revelry.

....

....

....

....

....

....

Summer Solstice

(General) *Great Goddess, mother of us all who brings us abundance and growth and causes the land to burst forth into blossom, I call you here on this day of the Summer Solstice!*

Great God, father of us all who is the sun up above and the greening of the land, I call you here on this day of the Summer Solstice!

(Specific) *Beloved Aine, lady of the summer and bringer of prosperity and abundance, share with me your gifts on this Summer Solstice day and guide me with your gentle wisdom. Let your light warm my heart and brighten my spirit. So mote it be.*

Strong Belinos, lord of the sun, whose powerful rays bring healing and strength, share with me your gifts on this Summer Solstice day and empower me with your energy. So mote it be.

Lammas

(General) *Great Goddess, you who are called Demeter and Ceres and Corn Woman, bring me your energy for growth and abundance on this blessed Lammas day.*

Great God, lord of the animals and the fields and the harvest, bring me your energy for growth and abundance on this blessed Lammas day.

(Specific) *I invoke you, Demeter, lady of the grain, goddess of the harvest, bountiful mother who provides us with nourishment for our souls and food for our tables. Be with me now as I celebrate your power and your gifts. So mote it be.*

I invoke you, Lugh, lord of the sun, god of the fields, bringer of light, warmth, and abundance. Be with me now as I celebrate your power and your gifts. So mote it be.

(General) *O Goddess, blessed lady of the bright day and mistress of the dark night who balances all of creation in the circle of your arms, come to me on this day of balance and autumnal glory.*

O God, sun to the Goddess's moon, strength to her compassion, masculine to her feminine, come to me on this day and show me the way to balance all that lies within and without.

(Specific) *Lovely Demeter who brings forth the crops and causes the grain to grow, join me now in this rite as I give thanks for all the bounty of the season.*

O great Dionysus, god of wine, god of joy and celebration, join me now in this rite of thanksgiving and abundance.

....

....

....

....

....

....

....

(General) *Dark Goddess who rules the night and the cold season, come to me and help me pierce the veil so I might see clearly and speak to those who have gone before.*

Wild God who rules the beasts and the forest, come to me and lend me your protection as I walk the shadowed ways.

(Specific) *I call to thee, Hecate, you who are crone and grandmother to us all! Dark and powerful, you watch over beginnings and endings. Come to me on this night that is both the end of one year and the beginning of the other, and guide my steps at the crossroads of the year.*

I call to thee, Cernunnos! Lord of the wild things, horned god who watches over both hunter and hunted, watch over me this night as I celebrate Samhain.

Yule/Winter Solstice

(General) *Great Goddess, I welcome you to my
celebration of the Winter Solstice and ask that you bring
your warmth and light on this cold, dark night.*

*Great God, I welcome you to my celebration of the Winter
Solstice and welcome your return, bringing the sun with you.*

(Specific) *Mother Holle, guardian of house and
home, watch over me and mine on this day of the
Winter Solstice. Welcome and blessed be.*

*Holly King, I thank you for ruling over the last half
of the year and the gifts that you brought me, and I
welcome your brother, the Oak King, as he takes up his
reign for the season to come. Blessings to you both.*

....

....

....

....

....

....

All-Purpose Invocation

*Great Goddess/great God, I greet you
and welcome you to my sacred circle.
Welcome and blessed be.*

....

....

....

....

....

....

....

....

....

....

....

....

....

....

....

....

....

....

....

Quarter Calls

Quarter calls are a way of inviting the powers of the four quarters: north, east, south, and west. In most modern practices, these are linked with specific elements, traits, and colors. These things are often mentioned when calling the quarters, as you will see in the examples below. We call in the quarters to protect us and watch over our magical space, as well as to lend us their gifts.

Most witches do quarter calls as a part of the circle casting at the beginning of a formal ritual. Some also call the quarters for even minor work. This is up to you, but as with much of Witch-craft, if you are just beginning your practice and still working on maintaining focus, you might find it helpful. Don't forget that if you start off by calling the quarters, you have to finish off by dismissing them. Dismissing the quarters is easy. You can say more or less what you did to start, but instead of inviting them in, you thank them for coming, or you can simply acknowledge them and thank them. Just as when you invoke the God and/or Goddess, most people light candles when they call the quarters.

The Four Quarters and Their Associations

For most Wiccans and many modern witches, the associations for the four quarters are as follows:

East: The element of air. The color yellow. The mind, intellect, thought, ideas, knowledge, communication. Air images include everything from a mild spring breeze to a wild tornado. Can be represented by incense or sage (anything that produces smoke) or a feather. Also associated with dawn and spring.

South: The element of fire. The color red or orange. Passion, courage, energy, creativity. Fire images include smoldering coals, flickering flames, and erupting volcanoes. Usually represented by a candle, but you can also use battery powered candles (if you are someplace where you can't have a live flame) or even a hunk of coal or a piece of obsidian. Also associated with noon and summer.

West: The element of water. The color blue. Emotions, intuition, cleansing, healing, purification. Water images include ponds, lakes, rivers, and oceans, but also a drop of rain or a torrential storm. Represented by water, usually in a bowl or chalice, but you can also use a shell. Also associated with twilight and autumn.

North: The element of earth. The color green or brown. Grounding, the material world, prosperity, growth, the physical body. Earth images include fields, forests, the ground beneath your feet, the earth itself. Often represented by a rock or crystal but sometimes by salt. Also associated with midnight and winter.

The various aspects of the four quarters are often utilized in creating quarter calls, but this can be as simple or as complicated as you prefer. For instance, at its most basic, a quarter call can be as straightforward as "I summon the spirit of air." Some people refer to the quarters as watchtowers, so you could also say "I summon the watchtower of the east, the power of air." Or you can do quarter calls that are specific to the time of year or the occasion, such as one of the sabbats.

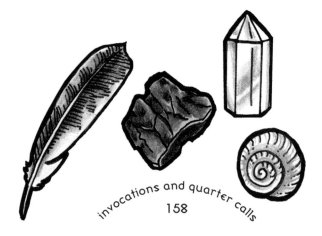

Basic Quarter Calls with Dismissals

East: I summon the spirit of east, the element of air, and ask that you guard me with the power of the sudden storm and hold me safe with the gentleness of the evening breeze.

Air, element of the east, I thank you for your protection and grant you leave to go.

South: I summon the spirit of the south, the element of fire, and ask that you guard me with the power of the roaring flame and warm me with the softly fading ember.

Fire, element of the south, I thank you for your protection and grant you leave to go.

West: I summon the spirit of the west, the element of water, and ask that you guard me with the power of the ocean waves and hold me safe like the waters of the mother we all come from.

Water, element of the west, I thank you for your protection and grant you leave to go.

North: I summon the spirit of the north, the element of earth, and ask that you guard me with the strength of the land beneath my feet and hold me like soil that nurtures the smallest seed.

Earth, element of the north, I thank you for your protection and grant you leave to go.

Quarter Calls for Spring

East: I call the watchtower of the east, the spirit of air. Help me to keep my mind clear and open and blow in the winds of positive change. Come now and guard my circle.

Spirit of air, I thank you for your presence here in my circle. You are free to go, though your essence is always with me. Blessed be.

South: I call the watchtower of the south, spirit of fire. Element of passion and transformation, help me to make the choices that will lead to greater health and success in the months ahead. Come now and guard my circle.

Spirit of fire, I thank you for your presence here in my circle. You are free to go, though your essence is always with me. Blessed be.

West: I call the watchtower of the west, spirit of water. Open my heart to love, my body to healing, and my mind to wisdom from within and without. Come now and guard my circle.

Spirit of water, I thank you for your presence here in my circle. You are free to go, though your essence is always with me. Blessed be.

North: I call the watchtower of the north, spirit of earth. Nourish and ground me; help me to connect to all the hidden strength inside myself. Come now and guard my circle.

Spirit of earth, I thank you for your presence here in my circle. You are free to go, though your essence is always with me. Blessed be.

East: I summon and invoke the east, power of air. Come join me in my circle, bringing the sound of laughter and a sweet summer breeze to blow away all my troubles. Welcome and blessed be.

South: I summon and invoke the south, power of fire. Come join me in my circle, bringing passion and warmth. Welcome and blessed be.

West: I summon and invoke the west, power of water. Come join me in my circle, bringing flexibility and washing away negativity and fear. Welcome and blessed be.

North: I summon and invoke the north, power of earth. Come join me in my circle, bringing strength and grounding me for the day ahead. Welcome and blessed be.

East: I call the watchtower of the east, the power of air, to blow away confusion like the fallen leaves and bring in clarity on the powerful autumn winds.

South: I call the watchtower of the south, the power of fire, to burn away the fear and the darkness, bringing the warmth and light of an autumn bonfire.

West: I call the watchtower of the west, the power of water, to wash away stress and tension, bringing serenity and peace with the rains that cleanse.

North: I call the watchtower of the north, the power of earth, to ground and center me with the land that always changes and yet stays the same.

....

....

....

....

....

....

....

....

....

....

....

....

These would be appropriate for Imbolc, for instance, or any winter full moon:

East: I look to the east and invoke the power of air—cold breezes that chill the body, yet blow away the cobwebs of the year behind us. With the coming of the light, may you bring me clarity and creativity.

South: I look to the south and invoke the power of fire— the warmth of hearth and home that shelters me from the winter cold outside. With the coming of the light, may you bring me passion to warm my life in the seasons ahead.

West: I look to the west and invoke the power of water— perfect crystals of water frozen into snow, each one different from the rest. With the coming of the light, may you help me to become more comfortable with my own individuality.

North: I turn to the north and invoke the power of earth—frozen beneath me now, yet hiding, still unseen, the first small stirrings of life, readying itself for the warmth ahead. With the coming of the light, may you help me give birth to the seeds of new beginnings that lie within me.

● ● ● ● ● ● ● ●

Note that any of these can be changed and adapted to suit whatever occasion you wish to use them for. You can also use them to inspire your own quarter calls, which you can write down in this section.

Classic Dismissal

One of the simplest and most traditional ways to either dismiss the quarters or say goodbye to the God and Goddess at the end of a ritual is this: "Stay if you will, go if you must; in perfect love and perfect trust. So mote it be."

Spells

Traditionally, the most valuable part of a witch's Book of Shadows was the collection of spells. Some of these might have been passed down from a teacher or high priestess or even a family member. Others might be ones the witch created for personal use. These days, they might even include spells found in books or online.

Either way, these spells are the heart and soul of a witch's practice, far more important than a list of herbs or stones. These are the witch's true treasure. In the early days, they were rarely shared outside a coven, but today most of us are more comfortable about passing on the spells we use to others who might need them.

There are a number of general spells that most magical practitioners like to have in their repertoire. These include the most commonly used types, such as healing, protection, prosperity, and love, but there is literally no limit to the things you can write spells for. I wrote a spell book that included spells for jerk avoidance (very handy at conferences) and potty training (I think that one is self-explanatory).

If you have a need, you can come up with a spell to help you deal with it.

Keep in mind that spells, while they can have amazing results, still require your focus, energy, and the intention to follow through after the magical work is done. But they can give your mundane efforts a magical boost, which sometimes makes all the difference.

A Few Rules

For the most part, modern witches only have one rule: the Wiccan Rede, which is "An it harm none, do as ye will"—and not everyone even agrees on that. But here are a few rules I think eclectic witches should follow when spellcasting:

- *Harm none.* Even if you think it is okay to cause harm with your magical work, keep in mind that there is a good chance for karmic payback. Just don't do it.

- *Never do a spell that will affect others—for good or ill—without their permission.* Free will is an important tenet of modern Witchcraft, and let's face it, you wouldn't want people casting spells on you!

- *Don't cast a spell for fun or to show off.* Magic can and should be fun, but it is serious business and isn't something to play around with.

• • • • • • • •

Don't worry if you aren't comfortable writing your own spells. Not everyone is a word person. On the other hand, try not to let the idea intimidate you either. It really isn't difficult, and a spell doesn't have to be perfect as long as it does what you want it to do. Spells don't have to rhyme, and they don't have to be long (although both things are good if that's what you like). They just have to come from your heart.

Many witches like to use extra ingredients, like the herbs, stones, candles, oils, and symbols listed in earlier sections. These things can help to hone your focus as you set them out and boost the energy of your spell by reinforcing your intentions. However, they are optional, and you can decide for yourself how many and which ones you want to use. The simplest spells are often spoken out loud with nothing other than your belief to accompany them out into the universe. If you have something large and important to work on, however, you might want to add some of those extras. Simply look through that part of the book and find the ones that suit you best (or, you know, the ones you happen to have in the house already).

You can also decide whether or not you are going to cast a formal circle, invoke a goddess and/or a god, and call the quarters. If you are working on a goal that is associated with a particular goddess, like love and Aphrodite, for instance, you might want to call on that deity. Or if you have a patron god/dess, that is probably who you will appeal to. Some eclectic witches just say "God and Goddess" or even call on "the powers of the universe," and that works too.

Spellcasting Checklist

Here is a basic checklist of things you might or might not want to use when casting a spell. You can use this to prepare, whether you are using a spell someone else wrote or one of your own. If you are keeping track of your spellwork, these are all things you might want to keep track of, along with whether or not the spell was successful.

Goal: The goal is what you are trying to achieve with your spell. It is important to have it as clear in your mind as possible when choosing or writing a spell; otherwise, you are less likely to get the desired result.

Timing: Are you going to do the spell during the full moon? At night or during the day? On a particular date or time or holiday? Sometimes these things are irrelevant; sometimes they aren't.

God/goddess/deity: Who, if anyone, will you be petitioning with your spell, or asking to help you with your goal?

Optional extras: These are all the items I mentioned before, like herbs and crystals. Make a list of any you will be using to reinforce your magical work. If you are planning to use symbols you aren't very familiar with, you might want to have them copied down on a piece of paper ahead of time.

The spell: While some people can just come up with spells off the tops of their heads, most of us do better having them written out ahead of time. If you are good at memorizing things, you can recite the spell by heart. I have a few I use often enough or have used for so many years that I don't need to have them right in front of me. But there is nothing wrong with having the spell written down or reading it out of a book just to be sure you get it right.

Lunar Love

Witchcraft is often centered around the phases of the moon. We celebrate the Goddess on the night of the full moon, and often our spells depend on the moon's changing phases. While you can certainly do a spell anytime you really need to, sometimes the phase of the moon may change your approach to casting it.

For instance, the waning moon—when the moon is growing smaller, starting the day after the full moon until the night of the dark moon—is usually used for *decrease*: that is to say, getting rid of things, or lessening them. The waxing moon—as the moon grows larger from the day after the dark moon until the full moon returns—is used for *increase*, so this is when you would do a spell to get more of something.

Take prosperity, for example. If this is the issue you are working on, you might do spellwork for getting rid of debt or unhealthy spending habits during the time of the waning moon, then follow up with spells to bring in more money or new opportunities during the waxing moon.

The full moon is considered by many to be the most powerful time of the month, and it can either be saved for your most important magical work or simply to connect with the Goddess. There are some witches who focus their practice on the night of the full moon and only do magic then. The dark or new moon can be used for banishing work or for quiet meditation.

Magic and the Days of the Week

Some witches believe that certain days are better for working specific kinds of magic. If you want an extra boost to your spellwork, you can try doing it on the day associated with it.

Monday: Healing, peace, sleep, purification

Tuesday: Protection, psychic work

Wednesday: Intellect and study, communication, wisdom

Thursday: Prosperity, business and career

Friday: Love, friendship, beauty

Saturday: Home, protection, banishing

Sunday: Success, power, spirituality

It's Elemental, Dear Watson

The elements are another important aspect of Witchcraft, and we often call on them during spells and rituals. There are four primary elements, each of which has particular associations, as well as spirit, which some consider the fifth element.

Earth: North, midnight, and winter. The physical body, career, and money. Usually represented by the colors green or brown. On the altar you might use a rock or a crystal or even salt.

Air: East, dawn, and spring. Ideas, communication, social relationships, and the intellect. Usually represented by the color yellow. On the altar you might use a feather or incense or your Book of Shadows.

Fire: South, noon, and summer. Passion, energy, creativity. Usually represented by the color red or, occasionally, orange. On the altar you can use any form of actual fire, such as a candle or something bright red.

Water: West, twilight, autumn. Emotions, intuition, cleansing. Usually represented by the color blue. On the altar you can use a bowl of water or a shell or a piece of sea glass.

Spirit: The fifth element is that of spirit. The five points of the star that form a pentacle are said to represent earth, air, fire, water, and spirit, with the circle around them standing for unity, or the oneness of all things. To represent spirit on the altar, use a pentacle or anything circular.

spells

175

Some Basic Spells

There are certain spells that most of us will need some version of at one time or another. Healing, for instance, whether it is for a short-term injury, a long-term illness, or on behalf of someone else (with their permission). Prosperity. Love (although not a love spell that would work against another person's will, of course; that's just rude). Protection. In an increasingly unsettled world, that last one seems particularly important these days.

Here are a few of the basics for you to use. Remember that you can always change the wording to better suit your own personal issues and desires. You can also add any of the optional extras from previous sections.

Healing

I call upon the air to blow away illness
The water to wash away discomfort and pain
The fire to burn away what no longer works for my benefit
And the earth to ground me as I strive for
healing in the best way possible
May the God and Goddess watch over
me and help me get well
Mentally, physically, emotionally, psychically
I call on the elements and the gods to help me heal
So mote it be

spells

Prosperity

God and Goddess, please send me prosperity
In all positive forms
May abundance and plenty be mine
May money and gifts be mine
May I have all that I need and enough to share
In the best, most beneficial ways
So mote it be

Protection

Great God, protective father
Great Goddess, mother to all
Protect me from accidents
Any dangers that might fall
Protect me from wickedness
From those who might mean me harm
Keep me safe both night and day
With the power of this charm

Love

I ask the universe to send me love
Both positive and lasting
In whichever form is best for me
As now this spell I'm casting
Love to keep me warm and safe
Love that heals my heart
Love both given and received
And blessed by magic's art

Book of Shadows Blessing

Some witches like to do a special blessing spell on new tools, which they often consecrate at the same time. This is the spell my group used on our own Book of Shadows, reprinted from my first book, *Circle, Coven & Grove* (Llewellyn, 2007). To consecrate your Book of Shadows, whether this one or one you create for yourself, you can sprinkle it with salt and water (to represent earth and water) and waft the smoke from a sage wand or incense stick over it (to represent air), and then hold it carefully over the flame of a candle (to represent fire). Ask the power of the elements and the God and Goddess to bless and consecrate your book for positive magical work, then say the spell. Alternatively, you can just use the spell on its own.

Bless this book
In the name of the God and the Goddess
Who guide my feet on the Path of Beauty
Let it be filled with wisdom and knowledge
Let me use it only for good
Let me share it with those who need it
Let it help me grow in my Craft
And in my life
So mote it be

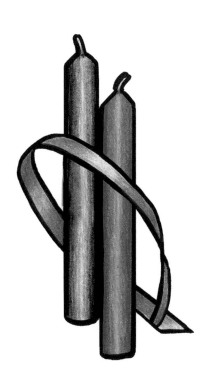

Some Other Handy Spells

There is no way to cover all the spells you could possibly need in a book this size, but here are a few other ones you might find useful. You can add others you find or create in the journal spaces or use those spaces as a place to write down the names of spell books you own and the pages of your favorite spells.

Calm and Serenity

We live in a tumultuous world. Who couldn't use a little more serenity?

God and Goddess, send me peace
Let the stress and noise just cease
For a moment let me see
Calm and sweet serenity
In the midst of worldly care
Connect me to the silence rare
Help me find my own true center
Before the world I reenter
Calm of water and sky so blue
Help me find my peace in you

Strength

This is something else we could all use a little of from time to time.

Goddess: mother, warrior, healer
You who are as strong as the mountains
As forceful as the blowing winds
As deep and unending as the oceans
Help me find my own strength deep inside
And lend me yours when mine runs low
Remind me that I am a child of the Goddess
And I am strong with your love and your will
So mote it be

Wisdom and Guidance

This spell can be used to open us to guidance from our own inner voices, from those who are close to us, or from the gods themselves. It can also be said before using a form of divination, such as tarot cards.

> *I open myself to the wisdom of the universe*
> *The wisdom that is already there and waiting*
> *Inside of me and from without*
> *I open myself to guidance*
> *I am listening. I am listening. Tell me.*

Balance

Use this when you feel as though your life is out of balance or you are trying to find the balance between two or more paths (like work and home or family and self).

> *Dark and light, hard and soft*
> *Left and right, on and off*
> *All is balance, balance is all*
> *Help me heed the measured call*
> *Help me find the path of poise*
> *Equilibrium amidst the noise*
> *Not too little, not too much*
> *Balance with a gentle touch*
> *Light and dark, dark and light*
> *Help me find the balance right*

Inspiration and Creativity

This spell can be used when your creativity needs a boost. If you can, say the spell right before setting to work on whatever creative endeavor you wish to inspire.

> *Like the spark of the firefly*
> *Elusive and bright*
> *Let inspiration illuminate*
> *And brighten the night*

Help creativity blossom
Like the heart's own flower
So I might see clearly
With creativity's power

Banishing

We all have times when we have things or people we need to banish from our lives. Sometimes they are external and sometimes they come from within ourselves. Keep in mind that if you banish something or someone, you might not be able to get it/them back, so this isn't an action to take lightly.

Banish now with witch's power
That which no longer serves me
Banish now upon this hour
That which undermines me
Banish now and for all time
Positive and with no doubt
Banish with this magic rhyme
The thing I'm better off without

Fast and Easy General Spell

Sometimes you just need a basic spell you can use for almost anything. When you're in a hurry, try this: "God and Goddess, hear my plea; send to me the thing I need."

Spell Kits

A spell kit is simply all the ingredients for a particular spell pre-assembled so they are ready to go when you need them. You can put your kit in a fancy box or a pretty drawstring bag (I like to use the organza ones you can see through so I can tell what's inside), or even a large paper or kitchen zipper plastic bag, if that's the way you roll. The idea is to have a magical tool kit or kits already prepared for those moments when you want or need to do magical work and don't have the time to root around in all your supplies to find the items you need.

Depending on how you do spells, your spell kit could contain any number of different things. I usually have three different herbs, small pieces of two or three different stones, a small chime candle in a color appropriate for the magical work the kit is for, a sage smudge stick, a packet of sea salt, and a copy of whatever spell I will be using. If you want to be really prepared, you could also include quarter candles, God/Goddess candles, a candle holder, matches, a vial of magical oil…the possibilities are endless.

Here are the four basic spell kits I like to have on hand: love, prosperity, healing and peace, and protection and strength. Use the spells listed here or substitute a spell you write yourself or a favorite by someone else.

Love: Rosemary, lavender, cinnamon. Amethyst and rose quartz. A pink candle. The spell below. As a rule, I don't like love spells that can affect someone else's free will, so I use a spell that only affects the one who casts it. From *Everyday Witch A to Z Spellbook* (Llewellyn, 2010).

I ask the moon and stars above
To open my heart to perfect love
Striving not, nor chasing after
But open wide to love and laughter
Hopeful am I and willing, too
To open myself to lover's woo
But while I wait for love that's meant
With myself I'll be content
I wish for love that's true and right
Filled with joy and shining light
I release all that blocks my way
And open my heart to one who'll stay

Prosperity: Basil, cinnamon, dill. Aventurine, green quartz, tiger's eye. A green candle. This spell:

God and Goddess, hear my plea
Bring abundance now to me
Let the blessings overflow
And good things come to all I know
Send me that which I desire
Help me lift myself up higher
Steer my path so I might gain
And true abundance now attain

Healing and Peace: Rosemary, calendula, lavender. Crystal quartz, sodalite, rose quartz. A blue candle. This spell:

God and Goddess
Grant me healing
Of body, mind, heart, and spirit
Send your healing energy
To mend that which has been broken
Center that which has become unbalanced
And sooth that which is painful
So mote it be

Protection and Strength: Rosemary, dill, parsley. Crystal quartz, black onyx, red jasper. A black candle. This spell:

God and Goddess
I call on you for protection
From any dangers
Manmade or natural
Intentional or accidental
From within or without
East, power of air
I call on you to blow danger away
And protect me from harm
South, power of fire
I call on you to guard me with a wall of flame
And protect me from all harm
West, power of water
I call on you to circle me with a river of safety
And protect me from all harm
North, power of earth
I call on you to ground me with the strength of stone
And protect me from all harm
I am protected
I am protected
I am protected
So mote it be

spells

191

Rituals

*R*ituals are the framework you build around a spell or magical working. That doesn't necessarily mean something complicated or long. For instance, if you observe the full moon by walking outside, lighting a candle, and saying a few words to the Goddess, then waiting in silence for her to speak back before blowing out the candle, that's a ritual. The simplest type, perhaps, but still, it has meaning and weight.

On the other hand, there are rituals that include numerous people playing out different parts, a high priest and a high priestess, casting a formal circle, calling the quarters, invoking the gods, and so on. And then there's everything in between.

What kind of ritual you use—if any—will depend on your circumstances and the particular occasion. I tend to keep things very simple when I am on my own, with an exception being very important magical work that I feel needs that extra oomph, in which case I might do an entire formal ritual. When working with Blue Moon Circle, we almost always do a full formal ritual because we find it helps to pull our energy together so that we are working as a whole.

There is no right or wrong way to do ritual, assuming you are not setting things on fire unintentionally, sacrificing your neighbor's prized chicken, or otherwise mucking about. So it really comes down to choosing which form of ritual works best for you at any given time.

Ritual Checklist

Like the spell checklist in the previous section, this list can be used to help you decide which elements of ritual you wish to use. You will want to start with the type of magical work you are doing, as well as your circumstances and personal preferences. This will help you choose the kind of ritual you think will work best: simple or more formal.

- *Solitary or group.* Group is usually more formal.
- *Special occasion* (usually formal) or *general practice* (as simple or complicated as you like)
- *Difficulty/importance of the magical work.* A simple everyday prosperity spell may not need a ritual at all; a spell to resolve a crisis might benefit from more formality.
- *Time and space.* Do you have the time for a longer ritual or are you limited to five minutes you can grab while your significant other takes a walk or the kids are outside playing? Do you have a private place to do a longer ritual or are you lucky to be able to recite a spell without being interrupted?
- *Personal preference.* Are you a "wing it" person or do you prefer to have everything organized and set up ahead of time?

Once you have answered these questions, you should have a pretty good idea of whether you want to simply light a candle, pull out all the stops, or do something in between. Then you can pick and choose from the ritual elements listed next.

Ritual Elements

There are as many different styles and formats for ritual as there are witches. Many of us who were originally taught by those from a traditional Wiccan background have certain basic elements we usually use. Ceremonial magicians have others. Eclectic witches may have evolved their own ways of doing things.

The following list is based on what I use and have seen used, but it is by no means the only way of doing things. Feel free to make a note of your usual ritual elements. Keep in mind that you don't have to do every item on this list; you can pick and choose the ones that appeal to you most or that work best for the circumstances of whatever magical work you are focusing on at any given time.

Cleansing yourself as preparation for ritual. Some people like to take a pre-ritual bath or do some other form of cleansing/clearing of mind/body/spirit. My group passes around a sage smudge stick at the start of every ritual to help us waft away the energies we have carried in from the mundane world. We also pass around a mixture of salt and water in a bowl to symbolically clear and cleanse ourselves. When doing a ritual on my own, I use the sage but not the water.

Gather your tools. Assemble all your magical supplies and anything else you'll need for your ritual, including your spell if you are using one that is written out ahead of time, and cakes and ale if using. Don't forget the matches for the candles! (If I had a nickel for every time I realized I'd forgotten mine when I was about to start the ritual...)

Clear the area. Cleanse and clear the area to prepare it for being used as sacred space. This can be done by sweeping the circle space (with a broom reserved for magical work); flicking water around the space using a small broom, a feather, or the tips of your fingers; walking around the space with sage or incense; or any number of other approaches.

Ground and center. Basically, this is a way to help you focus and keep the sometimes powerful energy generated by ritual from throwing you off balance. The simplest way to ground and center is to take a few deep breaths to call your attention to the moment. Then open yourself to the energy of the ground below you by feeling it coming up through your feet (or your tailbone, if you are sitting) and into the core of your body. Then open yourself to the energy from above by raising your arms and stretching up your fingertips or focusing on the top of your head. Pull that down to meet the energy in your center and take another few deep breaths. (Sometimes this is done later in the ritual during a form of guided meditation if the ritual is being led by a high priest or high priestess.)

Delineate the circle space. Some people have a permanent circle marked out with rocks or other markers. Others create a circle by sprinkling the space to be used with salt, drawing a circle on the floor with chalk, placing stones around the edges, or other physical methods. The circle can also be energetically marked off by walking around the area you intend to use and envisioning a bright light springing up behind you. When I am doing solitary work in front of my altar, I might simply turn in a circle, using my finger or an athame to enclose the space, envisioning a trail of light and power following where I point.

Cast the circle. You can cast the circle as part of the previous circle delineation. If you like, once you have finished marking the space, simply say, "The circle is cast." If you aren't going to do that part, you can just envision yourself surrounded by light and say the same thing. If working with a group, you may want to have someone walk around the outside of the circle space and say something formal, like

> *Earth to air, sky to ground*
> *I draw this circle round and round.*
> *Outside of time, outside of place*
> *Now we are in sacred space.*

You can also cast "hand to hand" by having one person take the hand of the person next to them and say, "I cast the circle hand to hand," and then have each one take the next hand in turn until everyone is connected. The final person would then say, "The circle is cast."

Call the quarters. See the invocations and quarter calls chapter. Quarters can be called by swiveling in place and facing each direction in turn or by walking to that quarter and lighting a candle if you are using a larger circle. If you are standing in front of an altar or have everything grouped in front of you, simply call each quarter and, if you're using them, light its candle. When working with others, you can either have one person do all the quarter calls, divide them between people, or have everyone recite them together.

Invoke the God and Goddess or just the Goddess if it is a full moon ritual. You can use one of the examples from that section or simply speak from the heart. Most people light candles for each deity, but there is no reason you can't just invite them in. I like to put offerings like flowers or something on the altar to symbolize whichever god/dess I am invoking.

Do the work. Once the circle is cast, quarters called, and deities invoked, you would then move on to the magical work. If you aren't doing any of those things, you would skip straight to this part. The options for spellwork are too many to cover here. If you are doing a group ritual, whoever is leading it will probably talk about the occasion (full moon, sabbat, whatever). As a solitary or in a group, you might do something to build energy, like drum or chant or dance. Or you might sit quietly and simply do whatever magical work you had planned.

Cakes and ale. This is a part of the ritual that is usually only done in more formal rites, but it does serve a couple of purposes. In a group ritual, it is another part of the bonding/sharing that brings the participants together. It also helps to ground you and help you come back to the real world after doing all the magical work, which can leave you energized and buzzy or slightly disconnected from reality. Cakes and ale is just a general term for food and drink—it doesn't have to be actual cake or ale. It can be a piece of bread or fruit and juice or water or wine—whatever you prefer. Keep in mind that if you are having a group ritual, you will want to keep the "ale" nonalcoholic if there are children or people with substance issues present. If I am outside, I like to place a little bit of whatever I'm using for cakes and ale on the ground as an offering to the land and the spirits.

Pass the speaking stick. This is obviously only for group rituals. In a group setting, the speaking stick may be passed around so that each person has a chance to speak without interruption.

Dismiss the quarters. If you called the quarters at the beginning of the ritual, you should dismiss them now. You don't have to do anything complicated, but thank them for their help and snuff out the quarter candles if you used them.

Thank the God and Goddess. If you invoked deity, be sure to thank them for coming and for any help they might have given you during (or after) ritual. Snuff out those candles as well.

Open the circle. You would do this in the reverse of whichever way you cast it to begin with. If you walked around the parameters clockwise (deosil), you would walk in the other direction (widdershins, or counterclockwise) to open it. If you visualized a circle of light forming around you, visualize it opening up.

Formal group rituals may be a little more involved, but they often end with everyone saying:

The circle is open but never broken.
Merry meet, merry part, and merry meet again.

Feast. Formal celebrations for sabbats are often followed by a shared feast. Even if you are celebrating the full moon on your own, there is no reason you can't have a feast if you want one, or at least a piece of chocolate. I'm sure the Goddess would approve.

Who Leads?

If you are doing a ritual with more than one person, you sometimes have to deal with the question of who leads. If you are in an existing group, that probably won't be an issue, although not all groups have a high priest/high priestess, especially these days. If you are a guest, you won't have to deal with this issue. But if you are part of a group of people who practice together, whether occasionally or on a regular basis, you will have to decide if someone will lead the rituals all the time or if everyone takes turns or if no one leads (although usually someone will come up with the ritual itself). There are no right or wrong answers to this, just whatever works for you and the people with whom you practice. Obviously, if you are a solitary, you don't have to worry about this. In that case, clearly, the cat is in charge.

A Basic Full Moon Ritual

Connecting with the Goddess on the night of a full moon is at the core of many Witchcraft practices. Here is a simple full moon ritual.

> **Supplies:** A white or silver candle in a firesafe holder. A quartz crystal. A small bowl of water.

This ritual can be done outside under the full moon or inside either at an altar, looking out the window at the moon, or anyplace else that feels right to you.

Take a moment as you start to look up at the moon if it is visible. If it isn't, at least reach your consciousness up in its direction. Feel the Goddess energy emanating from the sky above, then feel it coming down to surround and encompass you.

Light the candle and say:

> *Great Goddess (insert a particular goddess name here if you so desire), I greet you on this, the night of your full moon, and thank you for your presence in my life.*

Sprinkle a little water on the crystal and say:

> *As the water cleanses this crystal, so let your healing rays cleanse me of all that no longer works for my benefit, and help me move forward into this new cycle of the moon feeling refreshed and renewed.*

Hold the crystal up to the sky:

> *As this crystal comes from the earth, solid and dependable, let your strength ground me and help me move forward into this new cycle of the moon feeling strong and rooted, ready to face whatever comes.*

Hold the candle up to the sky:

> *As this light brightens the darkness, let the bright*
> *light of your love shine down on me and help me move*
> *forward into this new cycle of the moon feeling blessed*
> *and energized, knowing that you are always with me.*

Stay in the moment for as long as you want, then say,

> *Thank you, Goddess, for being with me*
> *tonight and always. Blessed be.*

Snuff out the candle.

One or Many?

Some rituals are written for a solitary witch and others are written to be performed by a group. It is a fairly simple matter to convert one to the other. Simply change the words as needed ("I call upon the Goddess" becomes "We call upon the Goddess" or vice versa) and change the actions as appropriate (if a group ritual calls for different people to call the quarters, the solitary would do them all; if a solitary ritual is done by a group, whoever is leading the group might add an introduction). Unless there is some task that requires a group to perform, almost all rituals can be done in either way.

Simple Sabbat Ritual

People celebrate the sabbat holidays differently. Not everyone observes all eight, for instance, and some people get together with other witches for some sabbats and do others on their own. The only real constant is that the focus is usually on the season and the theme of that particular sabbat. For instance, at the Spring Equinox you would probably celebrate spring, the returning of life to the land, and possibly rebirth.

Rather than write out an actual ritual, as I did with the full moon ritual, I'm going to do an outline of the basic ritual that would work for any holiday. You can simply fill in the blanks with whatever suits you. Figure out ahead of time what your focus/theme will be and what supplies you'll need. Here are the essentials most people will use, plus whatever is specific to the ritual you do. This is bare bones; you can add anything to it that you like.

Supplies: 4 quarter candles (red, blue, green, and yellow—or all white) and Goddess and God candles (silver/gold or cream/white), with firesafe holders to put the candles in or on. A sage smudge stick. Sea salt and water in separate containers plus a bowl to mix them in. Altar decorations suitable for the sabbat and/or deities you are celebrating. Cakes and ale suitable for the season. Any supplies specific to the particular ritual. *Don't forget the matches!*

rituals

Light the sage wand and use it to cleanse the circle space and then yourself. If doing the ritual as a group, pass it around the circle.

Pour a little of the water into the bowl, then add a couple pinches of salt. If you like, you can say:

> *Salt into water, water into salt. Wash away all*
> *that is negative and unnecessary, leaving me*
> *cleansed and ready to do my magical work.*

Dip the tips of your fingers in and anoint your forehead, lips, heart, and core (belly). If doing as a group, pass the bowl around the circle.

Cast your circle. Take a moment to feel the difference in the space.

Call the quarters and light the candles for each one.

Invoke the Goddess and God and light the candles for them.

This is where you would do your magical work. You might start by doing something crafty (like decorating a small pot with symbols of the season and planting seeds in it to represent the potential of the year to come, if it is the Spring Equinox), raise energy by chanting or drumming, do a guided meditation, or you might just cast whatever spell you are doing. If this is a group ritual, it might be more involved.

Once your magical work is completed, take a few minutes to ground and center yourself. Have your cakes and ale if you're using them.

Pass the speaking stick if it is a group ritual.

Dismiss the quarters. Snuff out those candles.

Thank the God and Goddess. Snuff out those candles.

Open your circle.

Tips for Doing
Magical Rituals

Here's the secret to doing magic: there is no secret. The truth is, you don't need vast amounts of arcane knowledge or a long, complicated ritual. If a ritual helps you focus your energy, by all means do one. But the most important elements to magical work are to have a clear goal, focused intent, and the faith that your magic will create positive change. Everything else is just cake—including the cake.

rituals

Simple Magical Working Ritual

The above hint aside, it is true that the elements of ritual can help you to achieve the focus and mental state that better facilitate magical work. There's a reason why religions all over the world have practiced rituals of one sort or another for centuries.

We often do our magical work within the framework of a ritual because it helps us to separate ourselves from the mundane world and the distractions of our lives and put ourselves into sacred space. This makes it easier to concentrate our undivided attention on the work at hand.

Here is a simple example of a ritual whose purpose is doing magical work (as opposed to observing the full moon or a holiday, although we often do magical work as a part of those rituals). For this one, we'll be doing magical work for prosperity and abundance, but this basic ritual can be used for any type of magical goal.

Supplies: A white candle (for the Goddess) and a green votive candle and firesafe holders for both. Herbs (basil, cinnamon, ginger, and/or peppermint). A green gemstone (aventurine, jade, or malachite) or a piece of tiger's eye. A coin (I like to use something fancy like a half-dollar or dollar coin, but a shiny new penny will do). You will also want something with a point, like an athame, a small wand, or a toothpick.

Optional: Sage smudge stick, 4 quarter candles, magical prosperity oil.

If you prefer, you can do the full ritual circle casting, as in the previous ritual. If you don't have the time or inclination to do a complete formal ritual, you can still waft the sage over yourself before you start. Otherwise, simply visualize yourself encompassed by a circle of powerful and protective light before starting this ritual.

Light the white candle and call on the Goddess (you can use the name of a specific one):

Great Goddess, I enter this sacred space dedicated to your worship and ask that you help me attain my goals.

Take the green candle and use your pointed object or the tip of your fingernail to etch symbols into it. These might include rune signs like Gifu (gifts), Ing (success), Jera (rightful rewards), and Fehu (money and material possessions), or anything that represents prosperity to you, like a dollar sign or the symbol of a particular form you would like your prosperity to take (if I wanted a new book contract, for instance, I might carve a book into the candle). You can also add your name or initials or any symbol that represents you.

If using the magical oil, anoint the candle with a drop or two, making sure to avoid the wick.

Sprinkle the herbs over the candle, making sure to inhale their scent.

Place the candle on a firesafe plate or holder and put the stone in front of it.

Take a moment to close your eyes and focus on your goals and desires, then light the candle and say the spell you're using. This is the one from the spell section of this book.

God and Goddess, please send me prosperity
In all positive forms
May abundance and plenty be mine
May money and gifts be mine
May I have all that I need and enough to share
In the best, most beneficial ways
So mote it be

rituals

Sit for a moment and then snuff out the green candle. Alternately, you can leave it burning on your altar or a table if it is safe to do so. If you wish to renew the spell, you can relight the candle without repeating the rest of the ritual.

Say:

> *Thank you, Goddess, for lending me your strength*
> *and your power. Please shine your blessings down*
> *upon my magical working. So mote it be.*

Snuff out the white candle. Visualize yourself letting go of the white light of sacred space and stepping back into the world.

Note: You can use this basic ritual and vary it to fit other magical goals.

Silence Is Golden

For the love of Goddess, don't forget to turn off your phone! There is nothing worse than getting into the zone of a ritual only to be interrupted by a loud ringtone. Silence your phone and any other potential distractions until the ritual is over.

rituals

rituals

218

....

....

....

....

....

....

....

....

....

....

....

....

....

....

....

....

....

....

....

....

....

....

....

....

rituals

Recipes

Witches really love their food. I sometimes think our rituals are simply an excuse for the feast that follows! (Not really, but still. We love our feasts.) So it isn't unusual for witches to include some of their favorite recipes in their Book of Shadows.

Pagan food can probably be divided up into three major categories, generally speaking. The first is "cakes," as in the food component of cakes and ale. These might be eaten as a part of any ritual or during a full moon communion with the Goddess that doesn't go quite as far as being an actual ritual. "Cakes" doesn't necessarily mean cake, either (although if you like cake, it certainly can). Much of the time it is some form of bread, which can include homemade bread, store-bought artisan bread, or rolls. Sometimes it is crackers or cookies or pastry, but I've also used fruit that is suitable for the season (chocolate-dipped strawberries for spring or sliced apples for fall). As long as it is something you can eat that will help ground you back to the mundane world or be part of your appreciation of the lunar or seasonal occasion you are observing, you are only limited by your imagination and your own particular dietary preferences.

Then there are the recipes that are used for kitchen witchery. Kitchen witchery is a way of integrating your magical work with eating, and it isn't reserved only for certain days of the year. Many of us who practice kitchen witchery do so often, whenever it is needed as opposed to on some special date. The wonderful thing about kitchen witchery is that no matter how busy we are—maybe too busy for complicated rituals—we all have to eat. It takes very little extra effort to add a little magic to the meal you were going to make anyway or to change up the menu a bit to reflect the kind of magic you want to do. Focus and intent can change the simple ingredients for a pasta dish into something that brings in prosperity or love.

Last but certainly not least are feast foods. These are the recipes we make for special occasions, usually shared with friends or family. Many group rituals, and some solitary ones, are followed by a feast to celebrate the occasion. This is particularly true of the sabbats.

Feast foods serve a couple of different purposes. Like cakes and ale, they help us to ground back to the mundane world. They also connect us with our ancestors and the witches and Pagans who preceded us, many of whom ate the same fare (although possibly prepared differently) at their own sabbat feasts. They give us a way to connect to the land as well, by focusing on the bounty that is available during that particular season. It is particularly nice if you can use some of the local fruits and vegetables.

Food sustains our body, and it sustains our spirit as well; the act of cooking for others allows us to strengthen and bring happiness to those we share food with. Most Pagan feasts are potlucks, where everyone brings a dish to pass. Preparing food for each other is an expression of love and brings us closer together. Some of the most joyful moments in my life have been those spent gathered around the feast table with my circle, eating from a plate that holds a little bit of magic from each and every one of us.

Cakes

Shortbread Cookies

These are simple to make, and you can add different herbs to them depending on the season. I like to use rosemary at Samhain (for remembrance) or dill (for prosperity) at the Summer Solstice.

> 1 cup butter
>
> 1 cup sugar (I like turbinado)
>
> 2½ cups plus ½ cup flour
>
> Optional: 3 tablespoons or less of whichever herb you are using, chopped fine

Cream together the butter and sugar, then add 2½ cups of flour and herbs. Knead dough on a clean, flat surface dusted with the rest of the flour until the dough begins to crack. Roll out until about quarter-inch thick. You can then use a cookie cutter to cut out shapes—round for the full moon, cats for Samhain, half moons or stars or whatever you like. You can also find pentacle cookie stamps to imprint the top.

Bake on an ungreased cookie sheet at 275°F for about 50 minutes.

(Adapted from *Witchcraft on a Shoestring*.)

Lemon Cookies

These cakes also can be dressed up by the addition of herbs. At Midsummer we sometimes sprinkle lavender on top (yes, it is edible).

    4 cups flour
    1 tablespoon baking powder
    1 teaspoon baking soda
    ½ teaspoon salt
    1 cup butter
    2 eggs
    1 cup sugar
    ½ cup brown sugar
    ⅓ cup sour cream
    2 teaspoons lemon juice
    1 tablespoon lemon zest
    1 teaspoon vanilla
    Optional: 1–2 teaspoons finely chopped herbs

Preheat oven to 350°F. Mix dry ingredients in a bowl. In a separate bowl, cream butter, eggs, and sugars, then add sour cream, lemon juice and zest, and vanilla. Add dry ingredients and mix slowly. Drop a teaspoon at a time onto a greased cookie sheet and lightly dust with herbs. Herbs can also be mixed in with the dry ingredients.

Bake at 350° for 10 minutes.

(Adapted from *Witchcraft on a Shoestring.*)

Easy No-Knead Bread

This bread is incredibly simple and quite healthy. It is especially nice for rituals where you want to pass a rough round of bread around the circle and have everyone break off a piece. It's also great for any of the harvest festivals, especially Lammas, since it celebrates grains. You just have to start it either the night before or early in the morning of the day you will be baking it.

4 cups unbleached flour

1 cup whole wheat flour

1½ cups rolled oats

⅓ cup brown sugar

¼ cup butter, softened

2 teaspoons salt

½ teaspoon instant yeast

2¼ cups water

In a large bowl, mix all ingredients together with your hands. Really get into it. Feel the silky flour sliding through your fingers. Enjoy the mess. Play. Bread is the stuff of life, and you are making it! Make sure the bowl is large enough to allow for the bread to become at least twice the size you start out with.

Once it is all mixed together, cover the bowl with plastic wrap or a clean cloth and let it rest overnight or for at least 8 hours at room temperature. (I usually shake my finger at it and say, "I want you to sit here and think about what you've done." I find that helps it rise really well.)

Once the dough has risen, turn it out of the bowl onto a lightly floured surface and fold it four or five times. Then put it in a lightly greased pan, smooth side up. The dough will be sticky. If you have a large oven-safe casserole or Dutch oven, that works best because the lid will steam the loaf a bit while it bakes. A pan covered with aluminum foil will work too.

Shape the dough to fit the pan or into a round loaf. Cover and let it rise again for about an hour, until the dough is puffy. You can garnish the loaf with some oats or sprinkle it with sea salt or herbs.

Place your covered pan into a cold oven and turn the heat to 450°F. Bake for 45–50 minutes, then uncover and bake another 10–15 minutes until it is a deep brown. If you have an instant read thermometer, it should be at about 205° when done. Place the bread on a rack to cool before slicing.

(Based on a recipe from a King Arthur Baking Company catalog.)

Chocolate-Dipped Strawberries

This is a particularly indulgent substitute for the traditional cakes and is easy to make even for the cooking challenged. I sometimes make these to celebrate the arrival of spring or for Beltane, when romance is in the air.

Fresh strawberries, washed
Good chocolate, shaved, or a good-quality chocolate chips such as Ghirardelli

Place the chocolate into a microwave-safe bowl and heat it carefully (in short bursts because chocolate burns easily) in the microwave until it has melted. This can also be done over a double-boiler on the stovetop. Dip the strawberries into the chocolate and let the excess drip off, then place them on a piece of waxed paper until the chocolate hardens.

Dark Moon Decadence

It is easy to make round cookies to symbolize the full moon, but if you want something truly decadent to use for cakes on the dark moon, try these:

½ cup good dark chocolate, shaved or chopped into small pieces

¼ cup heavy cream

Optional: extras for rolling the finished chocolates in, like chopped nuts or cocoa powder

Note: As long as the ratio is 2 parts chocolate to 1 part cream, you can increase or decrease this recipe as desired.

Place the chocolate in a bowl. Heat the cream gently in the microwave or on the stovetop. You want it hot but not boiling. Pour it over the chocolate and mix them together until the chocolate melts and they combine into a glorious smooth and shiny ganache. Spread into a pan to cool enough to work with (about 30 minutes to an hour in the refrigerator). Then use your hands or a spoon to shape them into rounds.

If you want to make this even more decadent, you can add a few drops of rum or your favorite fruit liqueur, such as Chambord. You can also roll them in cocoa powder or nuts.

Kitchen Witchery

Kitchen witchery is a form of magical practice that uses the innate qualities of various foods and herbs to add a magical boost to your meals. And snacks—let's not forget about snacks. And desserts. Desserts count too. For example, chocolate can be used for love or money magic.

One of the best aspects of kitchen witchery is that it takes very little extra time and effort. For those who can't manage to find an hour to spend on formal ritual, it is an alternative way to still get some of the benefits of magical work while doing something you would do anyway—prepare food.

And while I generally don't advise doing spells on anyone without their permission, I don't think there is anything wrong with doing a general "health and healing" meal for your family when the flu is going around or adding herbs for protection to a dish that will be shared by those you love. Cooking itself is a form of healing and love, after all, at least if it is done right.

Kitchen witchery recipes are usually chosen either because their ingredients already lend themselves to the magical goal or because they can be tweaked with the addition of herbs and such. Then you simply focus on your goal as you are cooking. For instance, if you are making a soup to increase health, you might add the specific ingredients for that and then stir nine times clockwise (deosil) while saying a healing spell or simply concentrating on your intention.

A Kitchen Witchery Quick Reference Ingredient List

This is not by any means an all-inclusive list, and many of these items have more than one magical association. For more information, check out the recommended books later in this section or go by what your gut says, which often works just as well.

Healing: Allspice, garlic, lemon balm, peppermint, rosemary, sage. Almonds, apple, cider, cucumber, honey, lemon, olives, orange, peach, pineapple, pumpkin, sprouts, tomatoes.

Love: Anise, basil, cinnamon, clove, ginger, marjoram, poppy seed, rose, rosemary, thyme, vanilla. Apple, apricot, avocado, beets, cherry, chocolate, lemon (all citrus), passion fruit, pine nuts, raspberry, rhubarb, strawberry, sweet potato, tomatoes.

Prosperity: Basil, cinnamon, clove, dill, ginger, mint, parsley. Barley, beans, blackberries, black-eyed peas, cabbage, figs, grains, grapes, leafy greens (lettuce, kale, spinach), nuts, pomegranates, tomatoes.

Protection: Basil, bay, clove, fennel, garlic, horseradish, mustard, paprika, parsley, pepper (both black and cayenne), rosemary. Almond, artichoke, blueberry, broccoli (and other members of the same family, including cauliflower, Brussels sprouts, and kale), chili peppers, chives, corn, cranberry, mango, onion, potato, raspberry, shallot, tomatoes.

Prosperity Pesto

The main component in pesto, basil, is a powerful herb that is good not only for prosperity, but for love and protection as well. So you might as well make a big batch! Pesto is a delicious green sauce that goes well on pasta but can also be used to season other dishes. I like to layer it on spaghetti squash with mozzarella and ricotta cheese in the fall. You don't even have to cook it—just throw all the ingredients into a blender or food processer. Plus it freezes well. Normally pesto is made with pine nuts, but they can be pretty pricy. Walnuts have good prosperity energy and are cheaper and better for you, so I tend to use them instead. Keep in mind that pesto is one of those dishes that you will adjust to your taste (I like mine with a lot of garlic), so the measurements listed here are just a starting point. To be honest, I never measure when I'm making mine. I just keep throwing things in until the balance seems right.

- 2 cups (or more) basil leaves
- ½ cup Parmesan cheese
- ⅓ cup chopped walnuts
- 2–3 garlic cloves, chopped
- ½–⅔ cup extra virgin olive oil (start with the smaller amount, then add more if you want it to be smoother)
- Sea salt to taste (about ½ teaspoon)
- Optional: squeeze or two of lemon juice

Mix all ingredients in a food processer or chop and mix by hand. As you add the basil, think of the leaves as representing dollar bills floating down, and invite prosperity into your life as you eat it.

Strawberry-Rhubarb Love Crisp

Strawberries and rhubarb are both associated with love, and they make an excellent combination when put together. The sweetness of the strawberries and the tartness of the rhubarb might even be said to represent both the realities of life and the way many relationships have a kind of yin/yang balance to them. This recipe also adds in a little bit of ginger, which is another love spice. For those who are pastry challenged, a crisp is much simpler to make, with no worries about a crust. Simply put the ingredients together in a baking pan and add the topping. Eat this with someone you love or make it for a feast and share it with your friends.

4 cups strawberries, hulled and sliced

4 cups rhubarb, cut into small pieces

½ cup plus ¼ cup sugar

1 tablespoon chopped candied ginger
  or 1 teaspoon dried ginger

2 tablespoons cornstarch

Topping
1½ cups rolled oats

1 cup flour

½ cup brown sugar

½ cup sugar

½ teaspoon cinnamon (or more if you really like cinnamon, since it is another love spice)

¼ teaspoon salt

1 stick butter, melted

Combine the topping ingredients by mixing them with your fingers or a fork. Put them into the fridge to chill.

Cook the rhubarb with ¼ cup sugar on the stove over low heat for about 10 minutes to soften it and get rid of some of the juices. While you're doing this, sprinkle the strawberries with the other ½ cup sugar and brown sugar and let them sit with the ginger and cornstarch in a bowl so the flavors can meld together.

Combine the strawberry and rhubarb mixtures in an 8×8 or 9×9 baking pan, sprinkle the topping to cover the fruit, and bake at 350°F for 50–60 minutes or until the top is crispy. Let cool before eating.

Healing Broth

I grew up Jewish, so I believe that chicken soup has magical healing powers anyway. You can make this vegetarian by using vegetable broth instead of chicken. This simple broth can be drunk on its own or used in other dishes. You can also freeze it in a large container or an ice cube tray, so you can pop out one or two cubes and drop them into any dish to add a bit of healing magic whenever you need it.

1 small onion or 2 small shallots, chopped

2 teaspoons olive oil

2–5 garlic cloves

4 cups chicken broth or chicken bone broth

2 tablespoons lemon juice

1 teaspoon fresh rosemary, finely chopped,
    or ½ teaspoon dried

3–4 sprigs fresh parsley, finely chopped,
    or ½ teaspoon dried

Sauté the onion or shallots in olive oil over low heat until soft, about 5 minutes. Add garlic and cook for another few minutes. Add all other ingredients and simmer on the top of the stove or in a slow cooker until they smell amazing. You can cook them for as little as half an hour or as long as half a day if the heat is low enough. Periodically stir the pot nine times, thinking of adding healing energy with every stir. You can either strain out the garlic and herbs or leave them. This is a great broth to use as a base for other dishes or to serve to someone who is sick.

··

Protection Broccoli with Mustard Sauce

··

2 shallots, sliced

1 teaspoon olive oil

1 clove garlic, chopped

1½ pounds broccoli

2 tablespoons butter, melted

4 teaspoons lemon juice

2 teaspoons course-grained mustard

Salt and pepper to taste

Optional: 2 strips bacon, cooked and crumbled

Sauté shallots in olive oil until soft, 3–5 minutes. Add garlic and broccoli and cook on low heat until broccoli is warmed through but still crisp. Combine the butter, lemon, and mustard in a bowl and toss with broccoli mixture. Top with crumbled bacon.

Recommended Reading

There are some great books out there that combine magic and food. Here are a few of my favorites:

- *Cunningham's Encyclopedia of Wicca in the Kitchen* by Scott Cunningham (Llewellyn, 2003)
- *Cucina Aurora Kitchen Witchery: A Collection of Recipes for the Novice Kitchen Witch* by Dawn Hunt (2010; this one might be hard to find!)
- *Witch in the Kitchen: Magical Cooking for All Seasons* by Cait Johnson (Destiny Books, 2001)
- *The Magick of Food: Rituals, Offerings, and Why We Eat Together* by Gwion Raven (Llewellyn, 2020)
- *A Kitchen Witch's Cookbook* by Patricia Telesco (Llewellyn, 1994)
- *The Wicca Cookbook: Recipes, Ritual, and Lore* by Jamie Wood and Tara Seefeldt (Celestial Arts, 2000)

....

....

....

....

....

....

....

Feast Foods

Any of the recipes in this chapter can be used for feast foods—in fact, there is really no rule for what can and can't be served at a feast. It is all about what you and your friends or family enjoy preparing and eating. It is traditional, however, to focus your food selections so they reflect the sabbat you are celebrating. For instance, Lammas is associated with milk and lambs. So you could serve up a hearty lamb stew or a creamy cheese fondue. At Ostara we rejoice at the return of spring, so your feast might include a salad with fresh herbs or some form of eggs, which symbolize rebirth and the season.

Feasts aren't limited to the sabbats. Although most witches don't have a feast for full moon rituals, there is no reason you can't do so. And there are plenty of other celebratory occasions, such as handfastings (weddings), Wiccanings (welcoming new babies to the community), and even passing-over rituals (funerals), which might be followed by sharing food. For the purposes of our Book of Shadows, however, we are going to focus on recipes for the sabbat feasts. Feel free to write down your own favorite recipes here too.

Imbolc Triple Goddess Cheese Dip

This deceptively simple cheese dip is so easy to make that even the most kitchen-challenged witch can do it, and it is surprisingly delicious. The three main ingredients reflect Brigid, the triple goddess many celebrate at Imbolc.

1 cup shredded Cheddar cheese
1 cup chopped white onion
1 cup mayonnaise
2–4 drops hot sauce (such as Tabasco)
Tortilla chips or bread for dipping

Mix the first four ingredients and bake at 350°F until gooey and crusty, 25–30 minutes. Best when served warm.

Spring Equinox Deviled Eggs

Witches tend not to believe in the devil (he's a purely Christian concept), but that doesn't mean we can't enjoy these slightly spicy deviled eggs. If at all possible, use free-range organic eggs (locally grown if you can get them). You will be amazed at the difference in taste and color.

1 dozen hard-boiled eggs
½ cup mayonnaise
1 tablespoon Dijon mustard
2 teaspoons horseradish
Paprika to sprinkle on top
Snipped chives to sprinkle on top (they represent the fresh grasses of spring)
Optional: 3–4 drops hot sauce (such as Tabasco)

Cook eggs and allow to cool. Cut in half and carefully scoop out yolks, setting aside the whites. Combine yolks with mayo, mustard, and horseradish, and mix until creamy.

Fill egg white halves with yolk mixture and sprinkle with paprika and chives.

(Variation on recipe from *Witchcraft on a Shoestring*.)

Beltane Sensual Salad

Most people think salad is boring, but if you do it right, it can be quite sublime. On May Day, as we begin to harvest the earliest greens from the garden, it is the perfect time to celebrate the earth coming back to life, along with a few sweet surprises.

> Small head of red lettuce, torn into pieces
> 2 cups baby spinach, torn into pieces
> 1 cup strawberries, hulled and sliced (you can use more if you want)
> ½–⅔ cup fresh herbs, including any of the following: dill, parsley, chives, mint, basil
> Sunflower seeds, about ¼ cup
> Maple-glazed or honey-glazed walnuts

Mix all the greens, including herbs. Top with sliced strawberries and sprinkle with sunflower seeds and walnuts. (I don't actually measure any of this—it's fine to just throw it all together.) You can use the dressing of your choice on this salad, but I like either a simple vinaigrette made from olive oil, balsamic vinegar, and a touch of Dijon mustard or else a creamy green goddess dressing. We are celebrating her, after all.

recipes

Summer Solstice Pasta Salad

There is nothing better than fresh vegetables still warm from the summer's sun. If you don't have a garden of your own (or it isn't producing much yet), try picking up some of the ingredients for this cold pasta salad at a local farmer's market or checking to see if your grocery store sells things produced by local growers. This salad is easy, you can vary the ingredients however you like, and it can be made the day before if you are going to be short on time. This recipe is one of my group's favorites, and I make it almost every year.

16-ounce box of rotini or some other shaped pasta. I like the spiral shape of rotini and usually make whole wheat so it's healthier, but you can use any kind you like. Cook according to package directions and let cool. Place in a large bowl.

2 large tomatoes chopped into about 1-inch pieces or a bunch of grape tomatoes, halved. (Hint: if you get multi-colored small tomatoes, it makes the salad look even more summery. I like to mix red, orange, and yellow to represent the colors of fire and the sun.)

1 large cucumber or 2 small pickling cucumbers, sliced and quartered

½ cup baby spinach or baby kale, sliced into small strips

½ cup chopped fresh herbs (I like to use basil and parsley, but you can also add mint)

¼ cup snipped fresh chives

½ cup sliced black olives

¾ cup shredded Parmesan cheese (can be omitted or served on the side to make this vegan)

⅓ cup pine nuts or sunflower seeds

⅔ cup extra virgin olive oil mixed with ⅓ cup balsamic or champagne vinegar and ½ teaspoon Dijon mustard to make a vinaigrette (or use the store-bought dressing of your choice)

Toss pasta with all other ingredients and then toss with vinaigrette.

(Variation on recipe from *Witchcraft on a Shoestring*.)

Lammas Autumn Corn and Apple Salad

The ladies of Blue Moon Circle all love salads, although we like to change them up depending on the time of year and what's in season. Here's one that takes advantage of the corn and early apples, plus the greens and herbs that are still in our gardens.

Cook 2 ears of corn (if you really want to get fancy, you can grill them, which gives them a nice extra smoky flavor). Cut kernels off husk and set aside.

Chop 1 sweet onion into thin slices, then cut slices in half. Sauté until tender but not soft, about 5 minutes, then add corn to the pan. Season with salt, pepper, and a pinch of Cajun seasoning if you like a hint of heat.

Add ½ cup sliced almonds to the corn and onions and sauté for another 2–3 minutes. Remove from heat.

2–3 cups romaine or red leaf lettuce, torn into pieces

Optional: ½ cup baby kale or spinach, torn into pieces (if you want a heartier salad)

½ cup herbs, chopped—I usually use basil, parsley, and chives, but you can vary this any way you like.

1 large apple, cored and chopped into bite-sized pieces

Salad dressing of your choice (green goddess is particularly nice on this)

Cook first three ingredients together as directed above. Assemble salad by placing greens in a large bowl and putting apples on top, then the onion/corn/almonds mixture of top of that. You can either toss it then or right before people eat it. It's like fall on a plate!

Mabon Layered Spaghetti Squash

By the time of the Autumn Equinox, we're deeper into fall and starting to crave richer foods that are warm instead of cold. Winter squash of all kinds are starting to come out of the garden and show up at farmer's markets. My favorite is spaghetti squash, which can be used instead of pasta because of the way its interior forms long strands. If you have vegans at the feast, you can make one half with cheese and the other without. This recipe can also be doubled if you have a lot of people coming. I don't actually measure anything when I make it; I just sort of throw it all together, so it comes out a little differently every time. The layers can represent the way we all start to prepare to burrow in for the winter, and getting the balance just right is suitable for a holiday that celebrates the balance between day and night.

1 large spaghetti squash, cooked (400°F oven for about 45 minutes; it's done when a fork slides in easily), then cooled enough so you can slice it in half lengthwise and scoop out the seeds. Rough up the interior so that the long strands are loosened somewhat. Keep the oven on but lower the temperature to 350°F.

Layer the following ingredients shallowly—each layer should just cover the layer underneath it, although you can always add extra of your favorites, if you like.

Pesto (I use my own homemade pesto, but you can use store-bought)

Ricotta cheese

Bruschetta or chopped fresh tomatoes

Sautéed onions and walnuts (make this layer while the squash is cooking)

Shredded Parmesan cheese

Place layered squash in a baking pan and bake at 350°F until cheeses are melted and everything is warmed through, 20–25 minutes. You can serve these on a platter with the squash acting as the serving bowls, and people can scoop out their own. Alternately, you can slice it into individual servings.

Samhain Rosemary Roasted Potatoes

At this time of year, our Pagan ancestors were storing root vegetables that would sustain them over the cold and barren months ahead. This makes potatoes a particularly suitable dish for the holiday, and seasoning them with rosemary is appropriate, too, because we use rosemary for remembrance, and Samhain is a time to remember our beloved dead.

- 1–2 pounds small potatoes (depending on how many people you are feeding). I like the fingerling potatoes, but small red ones will do as well. Little ones will cook faster and make it easier for people to take a serving.
- ⅓ cup olive oil (if you want to get really fancy, you can use duck fat)
- 2 tablespoons rosemary, chopped (fresh is nice, but dried is fine)
- 1 teaspoon coarse salt (sea salt or kosher)
- Ground pepper to taste
- Optional: to add extra flavor, you can use additional herbs, such as thyme, or throw in some chopped shallots or garlic

Wash potatoes, combine with oil, herbs, salt, and pepper. Bake in a 350°F oven for 30–40 minutes, or until a fork goes in easily.

Yule Sauerkraut and Sausage

The Winter Solstice is an especially good time to feast with friends, even those who aren't witches or Pagans. Have everyone bring a hearty, comforting dish to share or an indulgent dessert. Blue Moon Circle has an annual Yule dinner party with friends and family, and it has become traditional for one member to bring this dish, which was often served at her family's table at the holidays. If you have vegetarians, you can substitute meatless sausages. We make sure we have enough different dishes that everyone can find something they like to eat.

1 pound mild Italian sausage

1 medium onion, chopped

2 apples, quartered (you can peel them or not)

⅓ cup brown sugar or ¼ cup maple syrup

1 27-ounce can or jar of sauerkraut, not drained

1 cup water

Optional: ½ teaspoon sage

Cook the sausage and onion in a Dutch oven until sausage is browned and onion is soft. (If you don't have a Dutch oven, you can use a regular pan and transfer everything to a baking pan to finish in the oven.) Add all other ingredients, cover, and bake in the oven at 350°F for about an hour.

Warning!

It is never a good
idea to add herbs or
foods to a dish that
doesn't normally have
them if you are unfamil-
iar with the eating habits of
one or more of the people who
will be eating it. Be aware that
food allergies and sensitivities can
mean one person's treat is another
person's poison. If feeding a group, it
is a good idea to either check ahead of
time or have an ingredient list for those
who need it. And don't forget that there
might be vegetarians, vegans, or others with
special food needs. Ask people to tell you ahead
of time if they have food issues.

recipes
250

Correspondences

There are plenty of places in your Book of Shadows where you can find various correspondences for herbs, stones, and the rest, but it is always nice to have one convenient spot where you can look up the basics.

This is the most basic of lists. As you figure out which things work best for you, be sure to make a note of your own personal correspondences here for future reference or to share with other witches.

....

....

....

....

....

....

....

....

....

Healing/Peace

Gods & Goddesses: Apollo, Belenus, Brigit, Eir, Isis, Kuan Yin, Morpheus, Nuada, Rhiannon

Stones: Amber, amethyst, aventurine, bloodstone, carnelian, crystal quartz, fluorite, garnet, hematite, jade, jasper, jet, lapis, malachite, onyx, smoky quartz, sodalite, turquoise

Herbs: Apple, calendula, catnip, chamomile, dill, eucalyptus, geranium, lavender, lemon balm, peppermint, rose, rosemary, thyme

Colors: Blue, black (to banish illness), green (growth)

Rune Symbols: Uruz, Kenaz, Sigel, Tir, Ing

Love

Gods & Goddesses: Aengus, Aphrodite, Astarte, Bastet, Cupid, Eros, Freya, Hathor, Inanna, Ishtar, Isis

Stones: Agate, amethyst, garnet, jade, lapis, malachite, moonstone, rose quartz, turquoise

Herbs: Apple, basil, calendula, carnation, catnip, chamomile, cinnamon, clove, geranium, lavender, lemon, lemon balm, rose, thyme

Colors: Pink (romantic love), red (passionate love)

Rune Symbols: Fehu, Kenaz, Gifu, Wunjo, Beorc, Ing, Lagaz

Prosperity/Abundance

Gods & Goddesses: Ceres, Demeter, Fortuna, Freya, Proserpina, Saturn, the Dagda/Daghda

Stones: Aventurine, bloodstone, citrine, jade, malachite, tiger's eye, turquoise

Herbs: Basil, cinnamon, clove, dill, ginger, patchouli, peppermint, sandalwood

Color: Green

Rune Symbols: Fehu, Daeg, Othel, Gifu, Uruz, Tir

Protection

Gods & Goddesses: Bastet, Bes, Heimdall, Isis, Sekhmet, Thor

Stones: Agate, amber, amethyst, black onyx, carnelian, citrine, crystal quartz, garnet, jade, jet, lapis, malachite, moonstone, red jasper, turquoise

Herbs: Basil, chamomile, cinnamon, dill, eucalyptus, garlic, geranium, juniper, parsley, rose, rosemary, sage

Colors: Black, white

Rune Symbols: Thurisaz, Eihwaz, Eolh, Kenaz

Tristan Fox Mueller

Mickie Mueller has been a practicing witch for over twenty years. She's illustrated multiple tarot and oracle decks, and her illustrations have appeared in various Llewellyn books and periodicals since 2007, many also featuring articles written by Mickie. Art is a magickal process for her, and she uses various methods to infuse her work with magickal intentions. In addition to her art, she is also an author and presents practical witchcraft tutorials on YouTube. She makes her home in Missouri, where she and her husband, Dan, sell her art all over the world. Find more of Mickie's art at

MICKIEMUELLERSTUDIO.ETSY.COM

About the Artist